MATURE GRIEF

MATURE GRIEF
when a parent dies

Donna Schaper

COWLEY PUBLICATIONS
Cambridge, Massachusetts

Published in the United States of America by Cowley Publications,
a division of the Society of Saint John the Evangelist. No portion of
this book may be reproduced, stored in or introduced into a retrieval
system, or transmitted, in any form or by any means—including
photocopying—without the prior written permission of Cowley
Publications, except in the case of brief quotations embedded in critical
articles and reviews.

Library of Congress Cataloging-in-Publication Data:
Schaper, Donna.
    Mature grief : when a parent dies / Donna Schaper.
        p. cm.
    ISBN 1-56101-210-6 (pbk. : alk. paper)
    1. Parents—Death—Religious aspects—Christianity. 2. Grief—
Religious aspects—Christianity. 3. Adult children—Religious life.
4. Consolation. I. Title.
    BV4906 .S33 2002
    248.8'66—dc21   2002154782

Scripture quotations are taken from *The New Revised Standard Version
of the Bible*, © 1989, by the Division of Christian Education of the
National Council of the Churches of Christ in the United States of
America. Used by permission.

Cover design: Jennifer Hopcroft

This book was printed in the United States of America on acid-free paper.

Cowley Publications
907 Massachusetts Avenue
Cambridge, Massachusetts 02139
800-225-1534 · www.cowley.org

Contents

Acknowledgments

Pastors die many times. We "get" to die with literally hundreds of people. In my nearly thirty years of parish ministry, there have been easily a couple of dozen funerals a year. The funerals are not just rituals. They involve what happens before death in accompanying the person as well as what happens after in accompanying the person's loved ones as they grieve. To these people who have given me the privilege of dying with them, this book is dedicated.

Introduction

MY PARENTS KNEW MORE about how to bury their parents than I know about how to bury mine. They were part of a community, with communal memories and "ways of doing things." They did not follow orders so much as cultural instructions. Most people "laid Grandma out" in such and such a way. Children in the family saw her body in the living room. The presence of a dead body was normalized. This kind of "viewing" is just one example of the many cultural changes in our dealings with matters of life and death today.

I remember when my ninety-year-old neighbor died. She was Catholic. Of course, we planned to pay our respects at the funeral home. My husband is Jewish, and he had never been to a Catholic viewing. After we arrived, I told him we would go up to her casket, kneel, say a little prayer, and then shake hands with the surrounding family. He nearly passed out. He did it out of respect for the customs of the family, but many of us do not even know that such customs and patterns exist, much less how our parents wish to be commended to the next life.

My generation has known more change and more stimulation than any before it. When we chanted the self-righteous "Nothing Like Us Ever Was" in the sixties, we thought *we* were the source of our interest to ourselves. We were not. We simply lived in interesting times. On top of the enormous stimulation and choice and change we have known, there is every likelihood that people in my generation will have as much time ahead of us as we have already had. I could live to be 100! What will I do with my second fifty years? How will

I mature into that biological, emotional, and spiritual state, I wonder?

I might actually be shaking hands with maturity. But how would I know? I am still called a "baby boomer"—like a James still known as a Jimmy, or a Katherine still known as a Katie. The label infantilizes me. It conjures up my lost youth as though I had yet to lose it. What is maturity for a baby boomer? It cannot be just the difficulty I already observed, the math that progresses to a layered complexity. But surely, in part, it is that: maturity is difficulty survived and incorporated.

Our parents are living longer, too, though they may live with lots more than aches and pains, as modern medicine keeps them alive and in need of care. As parents die, we will be bereft both of instruction and of time and attention, just as we are facing our own middle age. We have to remember all that we have already been and done. Instead of a little past, we have a large past. Instead of a report card, we have a track record. Instead of a few clubs and an athletic letter, we have a resume that tells as much of the truth as we can bear. We have memories. They come with us, and they complicate things. Our parents are the links to these childhood memories; when they go, we have to link ourselves to ourselves.

I mused, at 50, on the mid-point of my strong and well-braided tether, wondering what it meant to be a grown-up. I know it does not mean what it meant to my parents. They lived then; I live now. Now and then do not have that much to do with each other, except in the long and deep view of things. I want to enhance the deep and long part and mini-mize the shallow and short part. I still want to articulate ma-turity for baby boomers. We may even lean into a new label, grown-up boomers, instead of just boomers. One of the keys to that maturity, I think, will be helping our parents to die well. One of the keys to maturity will be developing a culture to help us as parents die.

If the past is any guide, life is going to get both more difficult and more interesting. The past that will incorporate itself into my present is going to continue to have more heft, more weight, more ballast. I think people of my generation need to reflect and muse on maturity, so we can find out how to carry all this weight as lightly as possible. That way, when our parents die, we will not have to be so defensive about our past any more. We will be able to claim it as part of our present. My parents told me this, but I could not listen. In the cliché that deserves its frequent repetition, it was amazing how smart my parents became as I—not they—got older.

At the middle of our tethers, we are held up by the sheer weight and details of our own past. Our parents will not take that past with them, but they will take much of the support of memory we have known. We are all knotted up in memories like a ball of yarn that a cat played with. As our parents die, these minor confusions become major. Who are we now? Who were we meant to be, by those who went before us? Has the way we lived caused our parents to respect us? Are they glad they had us?

Parents have children for millions of reasons. Surely one of the reasons is to have a partner at death. This book may help us to be that good partner. Our children imagine that we know exactly how to help our parents cross to the other side. Our parents may have even told their friends that we know. And most of our culture imagines that we all know what we are doing, when our parents die. We may even know what to do at bedside and graveside, but we do not always know that we know. This book may help us to know what we may already know, and fill in a few of the gaps. It is a book to boost your confidence as your parents die.

Great pains are taken to assure the confidence of the public in itself. I know that I try to look as much as possible like someone who knows what she is doing. And, the worst of it is that I do, sort of, know what I am doing. If the secretary at the church needs to be replaced because she has stolen the collection, I can help. If a clergy person wants to divorce, I can help. If a pastor has lost his ability to preach, and is only 62, I can be useful. But all this expertise does not mean that I remember everything I am supposed to pick up. It does not account for the baldness in some of the tires I am using to get where I am going. It does not mean that the phone call announcing my mother's death will not scare *me* to death. Like the phone call that already came, saying "Daddy's dead," I am not ready. I may never be ready. But that does not mean that I will not have to act like I am.

Capability does not mean that we are not tempted by indifference, by not bothering, by just walking off and out of our own lives. Nor does capacity to deal with our parents' deaths mean that we are one-hundred percent capable. Rather, it means that we would like to be so, and that we intend to be so. Competence (imagined or real) does not tell the whole truth about me, or middle age, or life's destination, or road conditions on the way. My competence does not give a clue as to what happens when I hear Ella Fitzgerald sing on the radio, "Someone to watch over me." What happens is that I start crying. And crooning. And praying. And laughing. I take back everything cynical I ever said about the angel craze. I find myself amazed, amazed at a deeper level than I ever knew existed at thirty. Someone *does* watch over me. Who sent this song anyway? Who gave her that voice, anyway? How did my parents do such a good job as to make sure I knew at least that song?

The hunger for protection, for assurance, for certainty is as much a part of middle age as is the competence. That hunger increases mightily when a parent passes on. The hunger is one of many threads in the same skein. So are stress and salvation. Those are just three of the threads in my emotional tether. Say "heart attack," and I tremble. Say "cancer," and I can already think of three friends who are gone. When a parent dies, though, he or she collects all the deaths we have already known. And they also predict more, including our own.

Now that so much has already happened, I would be lying if I were to say that I am not afraid of what is coming next. So much has already happened! I would be lying if I denied my fear about the final acts. Who thought that I would sing Easter hymns in a pediatric intensive care unit for hours at a time, humming my own son back to life? I had no assurance that he would live. Who thought that my parents could survive all they survived? Who could predict how much protection they were going to need, even more protection than Ella's song promises. If anyone had forecast all this drama, I would have said "no thanks," I am not the type. I like comedies, not tragedies. I prefer the comics to the editorials. I am a list maker. I like checking off what I intended. I do not see why the car I thought life was has to run off the road so often.

I also do not understand how I can be a little overweight in a world where children are starving. I do not think of myself as that kind of person. But here, in the middle of life, looking at my own middle, I have to acknowledge that I am. I will always overeat and be undernourished. My father never took good care of his health. All this and more is some of who I am.

If all these things have already happened, surely more of these kinds of things are coming. Emergency rooms, car wrecks, maintenance delayed while speeding down the road, each is a pattern. I think the pattern is called life, tethered, middling, muddling life. It is also, upon reflection, a kind of maturity, maturity that has ripened.

And now we are what happens after we ripen. We are the good taste and the bad taste we leave behind. If faith is the consequence of our stay in the pediatric intensive care ward, we may have found something out about growing up. Love is not indifference. Love is the capacity to care. It is worth the effort. As our parents die, extraordinary effort will be required of us. No matter how capable we are, at the end we will be asked to give more than we have. That giving will be worth it.

One

Simple Grief

JANET WAS FIFTY-FIVE WHEN she lost her mother who was seventy-five. They were close. And the loss cut deep. Yet there was a sweet poignancy in it, too, that Janet could not at first explain.

Elizabeth had died a peaceful death, at home. Throughout her final days, and at the last, fresh-cut flowers had filled her room with scent . . . and there were wordless reminders of sunlight, gentle rains, and hours spent together gardening. As Elizabeth had aged, her garden went fallow. Some of Elizabeth's stock and all of her wisdom were transferred into Janet's garden in time. And so, though they lived miles apart for some thirty years, flowers became the symbol of their bond.

Within hours of Elizabeth's death, Janet found herself compelled to take a walk around the old neighborhood. Much of it was still the same as when Janet had lived there. When she had visited, the had walked a thousand times. Pieces of old conversations came back, and better than that, the feelings that came with those long mother-daughter talks. For every one of Janet's heartaches, there had been consolation. For her confusion and questions, a listening ear and solid advice. For her joys, a companion to celebrate with. When she arrived back at her mother's home, she wandered out to the old garden, now mostly forsaken and overgrown—except for one small patch of flowers.

Both women had loved Sweet William and became expert at cultivating this fragrant bloom. As it happened, this was its season—and Janet found herself looking through tangled overgrowth at a small stand of pink blossoms, a brave remnant of her mother's love, devotion, and skill.

Alone there by her mother's forgotten garden, Janet wept and wept.

At the funeral later, Janet let others speak about her mother. Words would have been too difficult to manage. But in her heart one thought kept returning, "How could I have been so lucky as to have her as my mother?" And then the sweet-poignant feeling about her mother's death came clear to Janet: Yes, Elizabeth was gone physically; but much of her life she had spent transferring everything about herself, sweetly, lovingly, into Janet. Janet realized that more than gardening or anything else in her mother's life, she, herself, had always been her mother's most important work.

Every Grief Is Painful

Janet's grief was sharp and real. Every grief is, in its own way. And yet it also has an emotional brightness within it—giving it the defining characteristic of what I term "simple grief." That characteristic is a buoyancy, almost a sense of triumph or celebration in the midst of loss.

Before I go further, let me say that by using the term "simple grief" I do not mean to imply that any grief is simplistic in the sense that it is emotionally monochromatic. Grief is actually complex, in that it is made up of a constellation of emotions—from sadness and anger, to relief and elation. The fact is, when we experience grief many feelings are vying for expression. We can experience a kind of emotional "log jam" and not know what to feel. And suddenly we can be flooded with anguish, followed by calm; then a lightness and humor can catapult us into laughter and relief. Being on this roller-coaster of emotions can be unnerving, because we feel as though we do not know what is coming next from out of our own souls, and we sense we are emotionally out-of-control.

And yet, some griefs have characteristics, or "marks," that allow us to return more readily to emotional equilibrium. So despite the complex feelings that flood through us during grief, some griefs are simpler in that they are easier to manage and move through than others. Simple grief will take us on a tour of pain and anguish—but again and again throughout its duration, and in the end, it returns us to the goodness that is left when a beloved parent is gone. What are some of the marks of simple grief?

Marks of Simple Grief

Simple grief is marked primarily by the experience of finding our emotional state more quickly flooded with positive feelings—even an elation that, at moments, outweighs the sense of loss, however painful the wound of that loss may be. In fact, because of this positive emotional flooding, the wound of the loss has a way of healing more readily. So while Elizabeth's death struck a deep wound in Janet—this was her mother, best friend, and mentor; a singular relationship that could not be replaced. Janet found herself buoyed in spirit by her feelings of thankfulness, and even joy, in the midst of loss.

It is important to note, of course, that the basis for these real feelings of gratitude and buoying happiness was factual, not imagined. Sometimes, in an attempt to hide from real and painful disappointment about a parent, we tend to idealize them upon their deaths, even telling ourselves it is wrong to "think badly" of the dead. This amounts, not only to superstition, but spiritual dishonesty and emotional suicide. In Janet's case, Elizabeth's life, her actions and words, built in

Janet a true and lasting legacy of intensely positive memories and feelings. Theirs was a relationship filled with genuine love, respect, accomplishment, mutual admiration, and delight. The emergence of joy in grief was genuine, the flowering of a lifetime of good seeds sown.

This leads us to a second mark of simple grief. When we are mourning the loss of a relationship that was more a gift than an obligation, more a blessing than a curse, the way through our grief simplifies. Even as her mother's physical presence left her, and perhaps because of the loss, Janet was suddenly, acutely aware of all the good things in herself that were placed there because her mother loved her well and gifted her with so many good things in spirit. Though there had been negatives in their relationship—every human relationship has negatives—what rose to the surface was not only good memories, but a profound sense of being "blessed," that is to say, a sense that her mother and her life were good gifts from God. Janet's sense of being well-parented in both the human and divine senses was strong.

Thirdly, simple grief is more easily worked-through because we quickly come to a settled emotional stance as to how we feel about the person now gone, and about his or her life. That is, we can decide that it was a life well-lived and that the relationship between us was good. That does not mean it was perfect or all that we wanted it to be. But we come to terms with its essential goodness, and feel comforted and at peace that it was not a misspent and wasted life.

One way we come to this settled stance, besides carrying a legacy of good memories, is when we and our loved ones share affection for the same thing. This may be affection for an object, or a place, or a set of beliefs, or a pastime, or another person. In Janet's case, she and her mother shared a love for the beautiful and gentle things, also for hard work and achievement. In the end these intangibles came together in their love for the same variety of flower.

All of these things added together, helped Janet to recognize the deep, lasting goodness of their relationship. And so she was able to arrive at a settled place in spirit: "Given that no one lives forever, and I was bound to lose my mother some time, I have a lot to be thankful for," Janet said.

In the end, perhaps the signature mark of simple grief can be summed up in this sense of thanksgiving and blessing. We may be thankful for the life of the other and that his or her life touched ours. We may have a sense that we have received a blessed gift by means of our association, accompanied by a sense that, even in the terribleness of this loss, somehow, mysteriously, good is emerging.

The Heart of Simple Grief

When in our grief we experience an abiding sense of goodness—thankfulness for one lost, a knowledge that we have been blessed—then grief carries in its deep heart a kind of unmistakable brightness. We find grief, ironically, surprisingly, good. Even bountiful. Even as its plowshare cuts the soil of our souls, from the wounds pour rich memories, bright insights into why our lives are good, or why we are gifted in the ways we are. Our grief is not the bitter and withering kind; it is bearing fruit in our souls. Out of our loss is springing a mature appreciation for the one we loved, for ourselves, perhaps even for life itself.

Because we are capable of experiencing more than one feeling at a time, and because emotionally-charged events can cause our feelings to change moment to moment, experiencing the death of a loved one with a sense of blessing does not mean we will not also have rage, or anger, or depression around our loss. These emotions, and dramatic shifts from one emotional state to another, are normal. But with all these shifting inner tides, it is helpful to know that we do have a sort of pole star. And if we want to walk through grief, we can choose as our ultimate spiritual destination the deep gratitude we feel for the life that has touched and blessed ours with goodness. And so we may travel through the difficult feelings, authentic as they are, knowing that beyond them lies the restful harbor of a better inner state. The name of mature spiritual destination for which we head beyond our loss is gratitude.

Always, Shadow

As I have already alluded, no grief is emotionally monochromatic. To this point, I have focused on the predominant sense some of us can feel at the loss of a parent who has gifted us with mostly good things. There is, of course, another side to simple grief, a darker side.

Sadness and even despair is the other tide of emotion that can suddenly rush in and overwhelm us. Just when we have firmly settled ourselves in the track, comforting ourselves with the solid fact that the mother or father we lost was the best in the world—all in a moment, the ground falls out beneath our feet.

When the sudden slide from sadness leads us deeper into the dark, down into despair, the open mouth of pain and loss and even panic, is overwhelming. Every survival instinct tells us to cling and claw to the sides of our souls to keep from plunging deeper. We clutch at safety ropes made of words and logic: "I felt so calm and accepting and in-control yesterday. It makes no sense to feel this way today." "I was so blessed to have been their child, and I should focus on good feelings and memories." "I cannot let myself get into this feeling, because it feels like I am going insane." The attempt to escape the opening pit of dark emotions, natural though it may be, is a mistake. It is unnecessary. Always, there is a shadow to be faced. And especially if we are people of faith, there is nothing in any darkness that can harm us.

A wise minister I know once asked a congregation if they

ever knew despair—if they ever felt like there was no reason to go on, ever felt flat-out finished. "Have you ever felt dead though you're alive?" he asked? This being church, and a place to confess faith, we all hesitated. But in a moment, heads began to nod. In fact, in that packed church that Sunday morning, most people nodded an honest yes.

"No doubt you felt hopeless at the time, isn't that right?" the preacher pressed. A second round of nods. "Ironically enough, the ability to admit, 'yes, I am in despair,' is our hope," he retold us.

What spiritual double-talk is this? None whatsoever. As the psalmist, in his wisdom, cried, wondering at the vast everywhereness of God, "Even the darkness is not dark to you; for darkness is as light to you" (139:12).

That God is there in the depth of every darkness is a "given" of faith. But what we say we know in fact, we must learn in hard experience. In matters of faith it is the only way. That this wise minister knew this truth, and taught us not to be afraid even of our dark despairs, was a healing gift. For this man knew from experience about the bottom, and he knew how at the bottom there is a turn: at the bottom we find that we have used our last bit of strength, and logic, and coping skill, and it has not been enough. There is nothing left to do but reach out. Reach up.

Here in the dark, if we stretch out a trembling, even reluctant, hand in faith, we find we are given enough light to go on, and, perhaps, the sense that we are being accompanied on our way through the heart of the darkness.

From the Depths

At the bottom of grief's dark side, if we are brave and willing to walk forward with our candle of faith, however small and wavering, we will meet the source of our dark terrors. We meet ourselves, small alone, abandoned, all of our childhood nightmares realized. There is now no nearby parent to come when we are weak, vulnerable alone—no one who truly, deeply loves us, who will stand between us and the devouring void. The little child in us never, in fact, dies; the spirit of childhood merely sits silent, waiting for all the adults to fail or vanish, and then it appears to do what it does naturally and best. It cries from the depths of the darkness for a power from beyond itself to come to its assistance. What can help us when we are in the darkness of our grief?

This is where the word simplistic applies. It would be simplistic to say God can help us in our despair. And though I believe this to be ultimately true, it is more accurate to say God helps and even accompanies us as we learn how to walk, literally, through the fears that we feel now that we are parentless and on our own.

Rituals and blessings are the two most significant spiritual directions we can "follow" to find our way up from the bottom of our bleak and abandoned state. How do we use these ancient spiritual gifts to aid us in our grief?

Ritual

Perhaps you are familiar with the traditional rituals and blessings of Christian spirituality. Perhaps not. What I am speaking of here is not the use of one of the church's treasures, but the creation of your own personal rituals and blessings.

A ritual is an enactment of a spiritual reality, including a statement about the goodness of God made tangible. It is a way to lay out a pathway in spirit that will help you, over time, face the overwhelming nature of your loss so that it is not overwhelming but manageable. In the Jewish tradition, mourners take a whole week immediately following the death of a loved one to "sit shiva." During this intensely focused week, those who observe this tradition allow themselves to be silent, to wail. They allow their loss, as we might say, to "sink in." Beyond that, ancient Hebrew wisdom tells us, it is important to allow for a whole year of grieving. We who are of the Christian faith would do well to ritualize our griefs like this.

During the week after our loss, for instance, we might visit a room in our parent's home each day and pray there quietly. Or, we might give ourselves the gift of one photo album per day to savor. Or, we might open a pack of letters, or "visit" the contents of our mother's purse or our father's workbench. If we have to clean out their house or apartment or room, turning that task into a ritual can give us a spiritual direction through grief. When we merely turn the physical tasks of life's-end into obligations, and drive ourselves nuts with them, we rob them of their sacred ability to help us heal and deepen and move on.

Beyond the initial weeks after loss, we might ritualize our grief by setting out over the course of a year to remember the life of our loved one. We might approach each holiday, or other important date, not with free-floating dread, but with the intention of enjoying our memories of the treasured times. Or, we can advance through a whole year by laying out a plan to go through letters, papers, and personal effects. Or, we might plot a course of visits to favorite places, or with their old and dear friends.

When a parent dies, a sort of graduation takes place in our lives. An invisible line is crossed; we enter a new phase of life altogether. For many of us, it can be important to mark that passage, because it means the acceptance of a new mantle.

One man I know, upon the death of his mother, who was the closer of his two parents, felt an urgency to rent a cabin on a lake in the mountains for a week. There, in his grief, he faced the reality that his mother had been the spiritual center of the family. He realized that since he valued these aspects of life he believed the task of carrying the family's spiritual torch now fell to him, a task he gladly accepted.

On that last evening of his retreat, alone at a campfire by a lake, he carefully lit a small torch and held it into the dark night sky. "I'll keep the faith, Mom," he said. And with this small personal ritual, he assumed her role. Like this man, we can each create a personal ritual, and it will help us in our passage through grief. Such ceremonies can help us mine the goodness of our parents' lives.

There are many "duties of death" around which we can create personal rituals to signify that passage, such as handling a will, distributing cherished possessions, and notifying old friends. If we take on these tasks unmindfully, we may become merely exhausted by the trivial, while we could be uplifted by the meaningful. Every task left to us after a parent's death may help us move through grief to a deeper place. As we touch the spirit and emotion of their lives, we touch them.

Does this sound like making work? The point is not, actually, to make a "project" of letting go and working through grief. It is to be present to our multi-faceted grief, to allow ourselves to feel exactly what we must feel about our loss, all of it, the awful, and the blessed. In this way we can allow, not our sense of loss but our good memories to fill the world in which our beloved parent so recently was.

Blessing

This work we are doing is not done just in the interest of facing our difficult emotions, important as that may be. It has another purpose. If we approach it from a spiritual perspective, we are coming to terms with the meanings of ours and our parents' lives. Spirituality and mortality are meeting in us—Why were they here? What were their contributions? Why am I here and what is my contribution? What blessings were given to us, and with what do we bless others?

We are, in short, if we are believers, coming face-to-face with God as he has revealed aspects of himself to us through our parents. When I was someone's child I was one person, coming into my own as an adult. Suddenly I am an adult on my own, coming into my own by facing the questions: What will my spiritual legacy be? When I am physically gone from here, what will I leave behind in spirit? Now we find ourselves at the point where we can encounter the blessing that is ours.

With our rituals, we have been handling our parents' spiritual legacies. The truth is, what we will leave behind us—what we bless the world with—comes out of what we have received: namely, that with which we have been blessed. When we experience simple grief, our question is how to mine the blessing bestowed upon us. What are we to do with the ore that fills the mine of our inner being? How do we honor, not only our parents, but our own life from this point on?

To ask these questions is to mine the blessings we have been given. Each shining, faceted memory of the goodness given to us reflects an image that is ours, not just to hold, but to re-sow into the world. Perhaps, we were given a love of language, woodworking, investing, the church, the workplace, the nursery, the classroom, the stadium. This love is now ours to sow into the life of another. Will we let the goodness given to us flow on? To seek our blessing is also the beginning of charting our course beyond grief and loss. We sense it is now "our turn." How do we move, with grace and meaning, to the head of the line?

Transition

Simple grief, the kind that allows us to own the goodness of what we have been given, moves us readily to the head of the family line when a parent dies. Because we are gratefully exploring blessing, we spend less time caught in angry—or sad—regret about what was not. Somehow focusing on the good relieves us of the childish burden of complaining about the imperfect. Nor are we stuck in blame for what will never be. What is, is good enough. More than good. Ignited with blessing.

Rather, we may find, to our great surprise, that our parents' passing is, itself, a blessing. One day we may begin to sense that their moving on has opened the way for us to move on, too. They have been the great, overarching trees in our spiritual and emotional forest. This has had its benefits and its drawbacks. We have been sheltered from some responsibilities, but by remaining in their shadows we have not grown. As we revisit the lives of our parents we of course revisit our own lives, too. Here in this memory is the spot where they kept the load off our backs, faced a difficulty for us, or handed us the wisdom and know-how that got us through. Their sheltering presence, now lost to us, has felt like a terrible loss. But isn't there another way to look at it?

If we look with the eyes of blessing, we may see in our parents' passing our own transition into fuller, deeper maturity. We must come to terms with that which is our blessing to pass on. We must come to terms with our own mortality and other limitations, too. Even our own death is very much involved with the deaths of our parents. What have we learned about the events of death from being close to someone who is dying? And how will this experience shape the way we approach the rest of our lives? The light of our blessing will tell us.

Family Legacy

Many of us will face this transition with siblings somewhere in the picture. With siblings come struggles. We move from the stratospheres of personal spiritual and emotional transition to hard earth. With difficult questions to ask and answer, our passage is tested immediately. Who is now the head of the line? Is it, necessarily, the eldest? Who will take upon themselves the various roles of our lost parent? Where—to be necessarily mundane—will Thanksgiving, Christmas, and other family get-togethers be held? These questions make for interesting conversations in most families, "interesting," of course, being a euphemism for such words and phrases as "difficult," "emotionally-charged," and "a pandora's box."

Among siblings, questions of family leadership and responsibility rarely escape derailment into conflict and competition. Even among the children of "good" parents there can be a difference in experience or perspective, just as there can be differences in opinion as to who picks up the mantle as head of the family.

It seems obscene to allow conflicts, squabbles, and bickering to arise when a parent has just died. Better, we tell ourselves, to shut all this down, avoid conflicts, talk about these things "later." It is as if facing and dealing with conflict upfront and head-on is "dishonoring" to the parent who died. Yet moving conflict and competition to the center of the table is much better than avoiding it. Perhaps avoidance has been our family's pattern all along, a force that helped form many of the shadows—of regret, disappointment, and anger—that we encounter in grief. It is better to admit there is a proverbial elephant in the room than to deny problems. ("Problems? We aren't having any problems!")

Even among children who had shared good parenting, and where grief is simple and life well-blessed, a new emotional and spiritual order must now arise. And if we are all to move on to full maturity, we must face the bumps and abrasions siblings seem always to inflict upon each other in the long life of passages that take us to more growth.

Each Life is Eternal

Each life comes from God. It begins with God, and has no end. Our parents came from God, out from the circle of eternity, bestowed with goodness, and in dying they return to God. Their circle is complete. And in between, their spirits splashed-down here briefly in a quiet eddy at the edge of the flowing river of time. Our lives began as a ripple of their lives.

One day, Hafey Krech, a member of our church, came into my office to show me a slice of Dade County Pine. It had the faintest of smells, like incense and rain. Its cut surface was made of circles of growth—a tiny dot in the center, surrounded by circles rippling out in other, greater circles. Each ring represented, of course, a year that this old tree had lived. Hafey had looked at this slice and saw in it a cross, which he has since made. It hangs in our church's chapel. But these circles of the tree spoke to me that day of something else. They spoke to me of good seed planted. Of the rings of growth that make a life. Of patterns worked into our grain by times dry and wet, tough and easy. It spoke to me of the goodness of life—and good lives I have known that have helped to pattern mine.

Simple grief, in the end, is about honoring the life that began and formed the earliest, deepest, best pattern in our lives. In our memories, in our rituals, in our blessings, we circle and re-circle that life, and realize how central it was, and still is, to ours. And then as we turn out to face the life that lies ahead, the people left to us and our care, we circle and re-circle them with the steadying, nourishing goodness that gave us our best strengths. And so life goes on; and so the circle is not completed, but extended.

And in time we find that our grief takes on a new quality and direction. By moving deeply, slowly, through our losses, by mining the goodness there, we are able to move on. But we are no longer as we were. We are new. We are not alone. The ones who went before us, and the God who sent them to us, go with us. And now we see what we could not see before, when they were here to cover the view. Life in all its goodness moves on ahead of us. If we let simple grief do its work, such passage to a new place in spirit is ours.

Two

Complex Grief

LARRY'S FATHER LEFT HIS MOTHER when Larry was twelve. Throughout his growing-up years, and into adulthood, Larry continued to make regular visits to be with his dad. But the anger and sadness in Larry's heart at being left behind were never addressed. He never forgave his father. And so the visits cost him considerable personal expense, emotionally.

When Larry's dad died, at sixty-two, Larry was wiped-out. He had just begun therapy and was finding for the first time that he might have a way to forgive his father. Now he felt angry and sad that, once again, just when he needed to have his father there, he was gone. What was worse, death now made reconciliation impossible, and Larry felt more like a frustrated little-boy-in-a-man's-body than ever before. Larry was left, or so he thought, with the intensely conflicting emotions of complex grief.

When Grief Is Complex

When grief involves more unresolved negative emotions than positive ones, we may be stuck in complex grief. Complex grief is characterized by residual resentment and dislike, along with the wish that these feelings did not claim our inner space. We would love to feel only clear and uncomplicated sadness appropriate to the loss of a parent. But that is not our legacy, and resentment compounds upon resentment. Why can't we be missing a parent who made us feel good, instead of one who has left us to feel so much hurt and confusion?

At the spiritual level, there is more hurt and confusion. Here we carry a deeper sense that others were somehow chosen to have a wonderful relationship with nurturing, building parents. Over time, this sense becomes a bitter ache, even, perhaps, a force as strong as a belief, the belief that others were given a blessing withheld from us. We may even feel cursed, specially chosen for abuse, neglect, or just ignored, overlooked, and insignificant.

The first thing we need to know is that complex grief is as normal and ordinary as simple grief. Life was not a Norman Rockwell tableau for many of us; June Cleaver was not our mother; and Bill Cosby was not our dad. Recently, I attended a month-long professional meeting of highly accomplished people, and one night when we relaxed and told stories from our pasts, the truths we spoke about were as common as they were sad and shocking. Among the twenty of us, most told about childhood sexual or severe emotional abuse. Only two had missed growing up without some fairly severe injury. One thing was clear: We were not as special as perhaps we thought, and the complex feelings we carried were far from unique. Nor are we alone in experiencing complex grief when a parent dies.

This complex of feelings is, of course, an extension of what we felt in relation to our parents much of our lives, now magnified by the fact that no chance will come again to clear the relationship and create the healthy bonds we long for. We may be hit, in fact, with the whole force of all the complex strategizing we have tried over the years to get what we really wanted. For years we tried hard to be nice and agreeable, to win approval or at least escape blame. Or, we tried the aggressive approach, trying to "hit the problem head-on" by confrontation and talking, or shouting, it out. Or, we tried ignoring the problem, overlooking it all.

Nothing worked. For all our efforts we found ourselves still wrangling inside with the sense we were stamped: Disapproved. Out of despair, we gave up. Or we wanted to give up. But even this desire was fruitless, like trying to wish away a physical plague. We could not peel, pull, or pry this "thing" off of us. It was as though we walked in a shadow and the shadow stuck to us. We continue to run into disappointment in so many of our relationships, perhaps most of them. Disappointment seems to be our destination. Is it any wonder we feel cursed?

And now the parent who had the power to curse us, and who, presumably, had the power to lift the curse is gone. For those of us caught in complex grief, there is a way to undo the curse. Yes, we have a more difficult path to walk through the tangled way within us. But, though we have work to do, the puzzle is not insolvable.

A New Beginning

It is in our power to pass through the sense of lost blessing to a new destination. We can come to terms, and move on.

Forgiveness is both our path and our destination. If we will not walk this path, we will forever be haunted by shadows of regret, sadness, and anger, those "ghosts" of our parents that linger in our psyches. The past will forever seep into our present. Forgiveness is the way to neutralize the negative energy of memories that are our curse; as well, the way to turn these energies into blessing.

Now herein lies the problem: We may feel it is beyond our powers to forgive a parent who greatly wronged us, either actively by abusive, or passively by neglect. It is not necessary, at the moment, to believe you can forgive wrongs done to you. Feelings may be too raw and overwhelming; forgiveness may seem impossible. Nonetheless, we cannot stay stuck in this situation. Any negative feelings allowed to remain static and unchanneled will bore into our souls and create depression and illness.

For those of us who do feel this intense negativity, the way forward is simply to acknowledge that we do not want to remain in a state of contempt. To acknowledge that we do not want to continue returning indifference for indifference, disrespect for disrespect, hate for hate. All we need to begin with is this desire: We can acknowledge our wish to neutralize their curse.

Beyond this we may need to be honest about the reason why we are carrying a sense of being cursed, or that we are being denied a blessing. We need to be honest, perhaps for the first time, admitting that our parents rejected something about us. They may have treated us with neglect, or with just the opposite: over-controlling attention.

Like Larry's dad, our parents may have walked out of our lives altogether and left us with a void.

As we walk out of complex grief, we will most likely come to the bedrock truth at the bottom of it all: Our parents did not know how to love us. Here, we may need to stop and dwell for a time. We may need to look long and deep into the pool of sadness—and maybe anger, too—that has gathered over a lifetime. We may also need to recognize that we have never known how to let the energy of these emotions flow out of us, because we have rarely acknowledged these feelings as live and real.

One of the most important steps we can take is to begin our grieving by grieving for ourselves, for all the pain and anguish of sadness and anger turned inward that has been our curse much of our lives. This is the reality we must face, or, in fact, we will never be truly free to move on.

Moving on . . . to Loving

We stare into the depths of our grief. There we see images of our parents' abuse of us. There we see images of their failures to love us the way we needed to be loved. We experience our-selves—as we have every day of our lives, consciously or un-consciously—as rejected and rejectable. Something about us was seen as defective. If we step back and recognize that we do carry just such a pool of long-accumulated sadness and shame, we do well to ask, "Why have these feelings been al-lowed to gather so long here?"

This may be the hardest step of our journeys through complex grief. It is the step in which we make an admission. Even if we have dodged the truth about our unloving parents for years, it is harder yet to face this truth: We have become complicit in keeping the curse alive. As we have matured, we have failed to deal with the issues that caused the anguish to pool in us. We are not children any longer, nor are we help-less, vulnerable, and weak any longer. It is time to deal with our lifelong losses as adults.

It is on this point that many of us balk, and feel thrown-off. We may ask, "Aren't the parents who wounded me the ones responsible for the complicated feelings of my grief?" The answer is: They were the catalysts, but the reactions they set in motion are now our responsibility.

This is the plain truth. And though at this moment you may wish to throw this book against a wall and rail against this truth, taking responsibility for resolving your complex grief is a task that can be done by you alone and no one else. The consequences for continuing to live with frozen blame, in unforgiveness, are just too great.

Complex Grief

We Continue the Patterns
Our Parents Began

Keri spent many years in therapy and support groups, dealing with the pain and grief of a difficult childhood, intensified by the fact that both parents died when she was in her early thirties, leaving issues unresolved between them. For years Keri's anguish seemed to go on and on, until one day her thirteen year old daughter confronted her in tears of anger.

"You're never home," her daughter blurted one evening. "And when you are, you're on the phone for hours with your support-group friends. All you do is counsel, counsel, counsel each other. And when I need you, you say you're too busy to help me. Well, I need support, too." That was the moment Keri was shocked into reality: We ourselves often inherit our parent's incapacity to love and be present to the people who need love from us.

A New Legacy

A parent can leave behind such a mixture: hatred and love, fear and security, strength, despair and hopeful longing. This complex mixture is all too common.

Where do we, living and breathing in the present, find the power to finish with the past? When we feel the blessing of a good past, and even some of the present, has been taken from us, where do we find the motivation to forgive and move on? We can find motivation in this fact: What is not healed, remains alive in us. Not moving on from wounding will only reproduce "them" in "us." Not only that, we pass on these traits to others in our lives. To find the motivation to do the work that lies ahead, we need only realize that letting this curse continue to affect us and spread to others is to let our parents have the final victory.

And so we say "no" to the past, and "yes" to a better future.

We become tough-minded and tender-hearted enough to love ourselves, even though we have not been well-loved. We join the great crowd of other under- or over-parented people, and carry on in every hope of keeping our parents' failures out of the spiritual gene-pool. In this task, we can be assisted, again, by the creation of rituals that heal us of the many and deep griefs we have carried for so long. In this case, I mean healing practices that we need to pattern into our lives, if we want to transform our legacy.

Substitute Parents

We can begin the conscious task of finding parent substitutes. We can make this part of a ritual that heals us. We need these parent substitutes in our lives to embody the love, generosity, and acceptance—the blessing—that our parents denied us.

We can find these surrogate parents in many places. Priests and ministers, friends, mentors, neighbors may all substitute. We can begin with people with whom we are in long-term relationships, and take the time to consider the goodness that comes to us through them, especially, the blessings that normally would come to us through a parent, such as wisdom and guidance, unconditional love, patient correction, encouragement, and instruction in how to handle the difficulties of life ourselves. Eventually, we may find ourselves so skilled at the practice of plucking parental blessings out of relationships that we can even spot them coming to us through even casual contacts, for instance, the towtruck driver who not only hauls our broken-down car off the highway, but stands by to be sure the mechanic is correctly diagnosing the problem and charging us a fair price for repair.

Partners do not make good parent substitutes. Theirs is a different role, more involved with the fire of our emerging dreams and passions than with our unmet childhood needs. And though a partner, indeed, can offer wisdom and guidance and the rest, we always do well to seek our parenting elsewhere.

Partners can help but they are often as threatened by complex grief as we are. Nonetheless, we need many people, including our partners, to be with us as we walk through complex grief. We need vital connections to others, because a healthy inner life is fed by good relationships.

When we manage loss of relationship with a new relationship, we can be very intentional. We can say to whoever will listen, "I am having trouble with my parent's death. It would help me a great deal if you would please check-in with me from time to time and ask how I'm doing. Please give me space and permission to feel what I feel. I may also need help and advice. I'll ask for these when I need them, and you can feel free to offer support and guidance, if you can."

For years, Larry was unable to marry because he was so deeply afraid that whatever marred his father also marred him. Many of us carry fears that we will reproduce our parents' weaknesses and failures. When Larry's father died, Larry had finally found a guide and a parent substitute in the person of a good therapist. Together, they were able to find the way through Larry's inner turmoil and move forward. Within a year of his father's death, Larry married. To his own surprise, he wept at the wedding because his father could not be there. With the help of a parent substitute he had turned a major corner in his life and stepped into his own adulthood.

Sift for the Bad

We can help ourselves move on by taking time to sift through the past, so we can clearly identify what was bad in a relationship. One way to "ritualize" this is to schedule a regular appointment with a counselor or therapist.

Many of us are left with a general sense that life has just been bad, chaotic, uncertain, or threatening. We have never isolated the specific things our parents did or said that created this lasting inner climate within us. And so we are left under the cloud of the negative energy they have left behind. Again,

I emphasize using a therapist or professional counselor for this task. It is unfair and unwise to expect a partner or friend to go into the depths of spirit that need to be plumbed in the dark mines of our complex emotions.

When we take the time to look carefully at our parents' negative effects on us, we identify and isolate the bad. Perhaps our parents made critical comments about our lack of intelligence or skills. Maybe they dismissed our interests and talents and made us feel insignificant. Or perhaps they criticized our physical bodies. The more specific we can be, recalling phrases, words, actions, and inactions that harmed us, the more we are isolating the cancerous tumor these wounding energies have created in our spirits.

Once we are clear about the damage done, we can begin to repair our lives. This we do by replacing negative messages with positive messages to ourselves, and by replacing hurtful actions with caring actions.

Face the Toughest and Most Shocking Truths

Lorraine made a shocking discovery after her father's death. She found all the love letters her father had received from his lover stored in his bottom dresser-drawer under unopened packs of socks. Immediately, she recognized the handwriting was not her mother's, and she could not bring herself to look at the letters for several weeks.

While she wrestled with the matter, we discussed the question of whether or not she should open them. "Hasn't he hurt me enough already with his constant criticism of me and Mom?" she asked. "Why do I want to know more?" She had known for years that her mother, his wife, was unloved in certain obvious, deep ways. There was a lack of attention, a lack of consideration, forgotten birthdays and anniversaries. She had not known of divided attention.

Eventually, she realized her inability to decide whether to open the letters or not was symptomatic of a block within her.

She was unable to express negative feelings about her father, because she had been intimidated by him. The thought of learning information that might push her over the edge, into open criticism of him or, more fearful yet, exposure of him, was more than she could handle.

Yet, rightful criticism and exposure of wrongdoing are tasks of mature adulthood. In the end, Lorraine decided to overcome her shock and face the full range of facts. When she read the letters she was furious, and a fierce anger helped to burn off the confusion and chaos she had known so long.

Sift for the Good

Not only do we sift through our past for the bad, and sometimes even the shocking, we can also sift and find the good. Even in the most horrible of parent-child relationships, there is some good in the connection.

Daryl was left with complex grief on the death of his father, who drove him mercilessly and never rewarded him with a kind word. But sifting for the good, Daryl realized he had always admired his dad's business acumen and because of what he had been taught, he had also become a fine businessman. When we sift the past for the bad and the good, we are developing the mature adult skill of discriminating. We are refusing stay in the black-and-white world of childhood, lumping everything about our parents in the "good" or "bad" bin. Instead, we are picking the good out of the trash and holding it up to the light.

If we do not sift for the good, we are denying the good that is in us, bequeathed to us in our upbringing by the same parents who bequeathed us so much confusion and pain. To deny the good is to deny ourselves and what is healthy and good about us. We might think of working through complex grief, then, as mining. We may sift through the rubble of the past, kicking our shins, cutting our hands, straining our backs against heavy loads of dark and ugly substance, but hidden here and there are precious gems, some good facet of our own identities, well worth all the digging.

This makes way for another mature skill, and that is the ability to see and accept others in all their mixtures. When we have not dealt with the deep layer of angry judgment formed by our past, we carry it into all present and future relationships. Sifting the good and bad teaches us that each of us is a blend of both positive and negative traits, and that is human.

Seek to Understand

Our parents were formed in spirit and emotions, just as we have been. Often this means they are the way they are because of the way past influences shaped them. They suffer their own curses and their own neglect. Their own inability to love us had an earlier origin than their own personal failings. My own mother suffered from a terrible relationship with her mother. Once, at an early age, she was saved by an aunt when her mother tried to drown her in a bathtub. My grandmother was later put into a mental institution. It is amazing that my mother can love as well as she can, though I still struggle with the deep wish that she had loved me better.

Move Closer to the Only Perfect Parent

Many of us are learning how to experience God's more excellent parenting in place of the deficit parenting we grew up with. Scripture tells us that God is the God of the fatherless, and the motherless, we might add (see Ps. 68:5). He can father and mother us in all those places where we were not well-parented. When we come to the God of grace, who has love and acceptance for us, we begin to heal at a deep-level from the injury inflicted and the deficits left by our biological parents. This is to say, if we want to move on from grief and move into mature adulthood we can do so, if we return in spirit to our first Parent. The journey "home" to God can be long, especially if the curse is deep, for then we mistake the face of our parent for that of God.

What we need to know, however, is that from God's side nothing stands in the way of our return. Not our grief, or anger, or indifference. Not our accusations or blame. Not our furious or sad questions: "Why didn't you help? Why did you give me these parents?" There is one condition only for our return to our heavenly Parent. We must come just as we are—complaints, hurts, confusions, the whole mixed bag of who we are. Then we find our greatest, deepest, truest welcome in the presence of the One who has been waiting patiently, for many years perhaps, for our return.

My Own Journey

My own grief for my father was complex. I was glad, at first, that he was gone. I stood at his grave tearless. Standing at my side, my daughter asked me why I did not cry. She was fourteen, and I sensed I was disappointing her. I know she will remember that I did not cry at my father's graveside.

My mother had left my father in June, the year of his death. It was not the first time. He was the kind of man who could not buy insurance for a car because of his road rage and his penchant for attacking the state police. Once when a trooper caught him littering, he slugged the policeman in the face. My father had also been unable to keep a job. His anger often was the cause of his dismissals. And so we moved every year from the time I was eleven until I was eighteen. My mother would hold things together, sort of, economically and otherwise. Daddy was often legitimately angry at things that happened to him in the garment business—like losing his pension at age sixty because they fired him three months before the vesting. This company had done him wrong in a hundred ways, yet we never could tell whether he was responsible for the circumstances that made him angry, or if "they" had done it to him.

For her part, my mother had always been the kind of woman who stuck with her man—for fifty-three years, richer and poorer. She always made excuses about what a terrible, impoverished childhood he had. He responded to her grace and generosity with mental and physical abuse. So when she left him the last time, it was for good. Three months later, her husband, my father, was dead. He died alone, and his body was not found for four days, when my brother discovered him.

And so it was, that we stood at my father's grave side, each of us in a private turmoil of complex grief. And in the midst of all this, the matter of a gravestone surfaced.

The gravestone was an issue because it raised in us the sense of confusion about where Dad should be buried. At his death, we buried him alongside his father, in Kingston, New York. The real issue was, we were a family without a sense of home or rootedness because of all the moves Dad put us through, an ordeal my mother hated. She blamed him for the fact she felt she had no familiar place to call home. What complicated matters was the fact that they had purchased a plot and gravestone years before, when we lived in South Carolina, assuming that is where they would be buried. And to make things even more complex, my mother's family had a plot in which she could be buried, since she had been on the way to divorcing my father.

But there was the stone, someplace in South Carolina, with both their names chiseled on it.

It took mother a year to decide. When she decided to bring the stone with both names on it to New York, I drove to South Carolina to pick it up. A part of me was furious that my mother would make the choice to be buried next to him. Another part of me was delighted. A third part of me drove the stone north numb with sadness that behind me was the place where they had hoped to be happy together. I felt all these conflicting emotions, and many others.

Complex Grief

It was this complex of feelings that drove me to some brink inside. I was often beside myself with an overwhelming feeling I could not name. I felt like I was sealed inside an airless jar, stuck deep inside a dark closet, covered up on a back shelf. I felt trapped, unable to escape, sometimes panicky, even shaky. This was when I had to find my own way through and out of complex grief. And through a series of what can only be called miracles, I was able to do so. More important than the outer events that helped to move me through grief were the inner movements. I was able to sift through the good and bad of the past and remember being part of a family that somehow remained close. I was able to receive the grace and know the presence of God, which is what always comforted me when my biological family failed me.

In point of fact, I had to come to terms with the understanding that I would never have the reconciliation with my father for which I had sought help in years of therapy. There was no longer any chance to experience him loving me instead of acting disdainful toward me, as he always had.

But in other ways, I have been able to work through grief, escape the sense of being cursed, and move on to new maturity. For me, that has come, ultimately, from relying on the love of God, not only for me but for my imperfect father. As I have learned to rest in God's love, grace, and acceptance of me, I have experienced love so much greater than my own, and it has filled the deficits in love in me. Love, the kind that comes from God, is itself a miracle, and it performs miracles. In the end it has made me able to forgive, and love. God's love has brought me the blessing I longed for.

Our Task

When we stand at the gravesite of a parent who has left us with complex grief, we experience a withholding of love and life. These were withheld from us. We learned to withhold them in return. Refusing to walk through complex grief, or not knowing how, we continue to keep from ourselves the flow of love and life we need. What we are holding onto is a curse.

The dark complications of our past will not disappear all at once, that is true. But as we move toward forgiveness, and let the love of God flow into us, we free the log-jam within our spirits. A healing flow of love opens, life itself opens, and wonderful healing starts.

Our real task, when dealing with complex grief, is to get free of the curse and experience blessing. A curse is the forecast of trouble far into the future. A blessing is the forecast of good.

We who are people of faith can experience blessing. We can experience it from the hand of our God whose Word rings with this promise: "Surely goodness and mercy shall follow me all the days of my life and I will dwell in the house of the Lord forever" (Ps. 23:6). Not the curse, but goodness. This is the legacy of everyone who comes home to the shelter of love and forgiveness that is the spiritual house of the heavenly Father. Regardless of the complexities of your grief, it can be your legacy, too.

Three

Bearing Weight
and Becoming Light

RECENTLY, A NURSE WHO WORKS in a local nursing home told me this story: "Not long ago, I'd just said goodbye to someone at the airport, when I overheard a father and daughter saying their own farewells. What I caught was their tone as much as anything. It seemed they expected these to be their last moments together. The man looked old and very weak. The daughter's eyes were shining with barely-contained tears. Riveted by the sheer intensity of the moment I felt compelled to pause, as the gate attendant made the final boarding announcement. As these two neared the security gate they hugged each other and held on for one last, lingering moment.

"The father said, 'I love you. I wish you enough.' The woman replied, 'Daddy, our life together has been more than enough. Your love is all I ever needed. I wish you enough, too, Daddy.' They kissed one last time, the woman turned bravely and disappeared down the ramp to the waiting plane. Then the father walked over to the window, just in front of where I was. Standing there, I could see he wanted and needed to cry. I hesitated to say anything, not wanting to intrude on his private moment. But he welcomed me in by turning and asking, 'Did you ever say goodbye to someone, knowing it would be forever?'

"His question instantly brought back the memory of expressing my love and appreciation for all my own dad had done for me. When we knew his days were limited, I had taken the time to tell him face to face how much he meant to me. 'Yes, I have,' I replied. 'And, forgive me for asking,' I ventured, quietly, 'but why is this a "forever" goodbye?'

"'Because I'm old and not well, and she lives so far away. I have challenges just ahead. And the reality is, her next trip back will be for my funeral.' Something they had said then came back to me. 'When you were saying good-bye I couldn't help but overhear. You said, "I wish you enough." May I ask what you meant by that?' A smile slowly pushed through the clouded pain. 'That's a wish that has been handed down from other generations. My parents used to say it to everyone.'

He paused for a moment and looked up as if trying to remember. The smile broadened, the look of pain was almost gone. 'When we said "I wish you enough," we were wanting the other person to have a life filled with just enough good things to sustain them.'

"Turning toward me, he recited:

I wish you enough sun to keep your attitude bright.
I wish you enough rain to appreciate the sun more.
I wish you enough happiness to keep your spirit alive.
I wish you enough pain so that the smallest joys in life
　　appear much bigger.
I wish you enough gain to satisfy your wanting.
I wish you enough loss to appreciate all that you
　　possess.
I wish you enough hellos to get you through the final
　　goodbye.

"With each phrase he added I felt overwhelmed, because I realized that, with just a phrase, well-known to both of them, and invested with deep meanings, this father had conferred all the love and wisdom of this marvelous blessing to his daughter. And that, as his final goodbye, he had chosen to turn a time of grief into a time of blessing. Tears sprang to my eyes, and I reached in my purse for a tissue. When I looked up, he had walked away."

The Wisdom of Balancing

This story adds to our understanding about the pathway that moves us on through grief toward greater spiritual maturity. It speaks to us about a blending of opposite truths, which, if we can achieve it, works a deep life wisdom in us. This deepening occurs as we acknowledge both the pain and angst of death as it separates us from those we love, and at the same time recognize that the occasion of death, because it is so profound, is one of the times in life when the potency of blessing is most strong. It is only blessing that can help us move on, not away from the anguish of our loss, but through the pain of our loss to a wiser perspective. It is blessing that makes loss "lighter," more bearable.

By invoking a family blessing, "I wish you enough," the man my friend encountered at the airport opened the way for both him and his daughter to make their burden of parting lighter. Setting her free to feel the weight of grief, and at the same time to go on her way borne up on the light of his blessing, was a great gift.

Many of us grew up in families that did not teach us the skills needed to grow through life's weighty realities. Blessing, which empowers the spirit, is the tonic that builds us within and gives us the means to face what is "un-faceable" on our own. Instead, many parents, because they are insecure, only know how to bind us to them, insisting in subtle or overt ways that we cannot make it without them. The message they convey is: "You are incapable." Or they insist, subtly or overtly, that we must help bear their anguish, loneliness, fear, anger, or their mission. The message they convey is: "You are terrible if you leave me on my own."

Of course, the urge to bind is not only one-sided. Perhaps it is us who have not wanted to bear the responsibilities of emotionally, spiritually, or physically-independent adulthood. And so we have bound ourselves to our parents in some vital area where responsibility on our part is required. And though grieving the one we loved is normal, is it any wonder we hang on in unhealthy ways sometimes by refusing or fearing to let go? Meeting the weightiness of life, ours or another's, is inevitable. Learning how to let go and moving on, by means of empowering blessing, is one of the wisest and most charitable actions we can undertake. How do we learn to bless ourselves when a parent is gone, and help ourselves move on?

Encountering the Weightiness

The weightiness of death, with its leaden finality, is indeed a heaviness difficult for the mind and spirit to bear. It is made up of part fear, part harsh reality, part drudgery. When mother dies, we will have to clean out her apartment and distribute her things. When father dies, his collection of old tools, or books, or recordings will be our burden. How will we tell Aunt Millie, who will be beside herself? And to whom will we turn when life's crises come down upon our heads?

It does us no good to avoid the weightiness of death. Or to minimize it with religious talk or folksie "wisdom," as in "The Lord gives and the Lord takes away. . . ." or "It was her time."

The burden within grief is real. And dodging it does little good.

At fifty-four, I was diagnosed with breast cancer. My daughter was just sixteen. It is not that I made light of the situation, but in a way I refused to face its gravity. "I'm going to be fine," I said blithely, brushing away fear and concerns. One day, however, my daughter got past my defenses. "I don't know what I would do without you," she said, catching me off-guard. With that one line, she undid all my shallow coping skills. Unwittingly, she tore the mask off. I was felled by the weight of my own grief and fears. What would I do without her? What if I became critically ill and needed her? And what about that lonely walk in spirit I would have to make, facing my own end, if the treatments failed?

In the end, it was good for us both to face the difficult weight of our grief and fears. We were like two women trying to figure out how to haul a grand piano up two flights of stairs, sure we could not do it, knowing we had to. Handling the interior weights we thought we could not move, lifting their spiritual mass, we found that, if we had to, we could.

I have spoken of encountering spiritual heaviness and learning to bear it as if it is something we learn in minutes, In one turning-point flash of realization that this is now our task. In fact, the heaviness of mortality is the greatest weight of all. And the weight of grief we encounter when a parent dies usually does not sink down upon us all at once. We are likely to encounter it again for years and years, for the rest of our lives, really. We will encounter it certainly as we experience other meaningful losses. We not only lose, over and over, people we love, but people who give to us bits and pieces of what we need to live. And every time we lose, we return to the weightiness that void places upon our souls.

As we age, interestingly, we are also likely to encounter the weight of grief even in life's wonderful moments. When a child marries, when a grandchild is born, we may be surprised in these moments by a small twinge of grief; again, we encounter the weight. The one we loved is not there to share in this joy. And somewhere deep inside, too, the voice of a new reality keeps reminding us that at each turning-point, life is steadily, relentlessly, moving on. The melancholy and reflective soul suffers most acutely, knowing now that all moments are fleeting. "Teach me to number my days aright," cries the psalmist (90:12), suddenly taken with intimations of mortality, not just as a universal principle and a reality he must carry.

Encountering life's heaviness can be a blessing. If we are wise, it can teach us to live and love in the moment, to treasure what we have now. Time and life are moving on. It is time for us to stop holding off on being content until we meet the perfect life and love we wish for. We may spend our whole lives waiting for an illusion to materialize, when what is materially right in front of us where we can touch it and talk to it is slipping, a little more each minute, out of our grasp.

Allowing ourselves to meet the difficult and sad in life is a way to gain, not only wisdom, but a vital connection to life and love.

Encountering the Lightness

What we know less well is a state I think of as "lightness," a state in which we have the capacity to bear inner weight. By lightness I do not mean a force in the soul that is the opposite state of heaviness, like two substances on the counterbalance of a scale, with one greater than the other. Nor do I mean the absence of heaviness, like having all good things in our shoulder-packs and nothing difficult. I mean a kind of buoyancy that gives our inner beings the power to bear and distribute heaviness: Think of the waters of a calm ocean, bearing up a massive freighter. Lightness speaks of the ability to bear with grace and calm that which is heavy and which we must bear. Lightness does not wipe out burden. Instead, it distributes the weight.

Here we come down to it: Mingled together with life's uplifting events is a calendar of darker days. Mornings, afternoons, weeks, months, seasons of difficulty. We do not know when these will come, and when they come we do not know when they will end. Hardest of all these darker times are the deaths. When those dearest to us die, we remember that we are mortal, and death will keep company with us throughout life, whispering, "Time is running out." We can let this dire voice fill us with deep inner dread, with terrors hidden in the inky darkness of our soul, keeping us small and afraid. Or . . .

We can develop a greatness of soul that overcomes all dread. We can let grief do its best work, and teach us that life encompasses both time and eternity. This comes when we stop ignoring the treasures of the moment and our physical lives. It comes when we stop being just creatures of time, caught up in life's endless muddle of details. In us, time and eternity can meet, enlarging us from within and giving us spiritual buoyancy.

Grief is the one experience that has the most potential to teach us the mature skill of holding these two realties, time and eternity, in delicate balance. Only the soul can achieve this subtle balancing act. It is utterly important to work toward spiritual balance. In this way we bring buoyancy to our souls, and then we are better able to bear life's great burdens with a lightness in our souls. When we open ourselves to this inner work we find that, even in our worst losses a kind of grace is at work. It is a grace that both allows weighty realities to press us, but also gives us time to absorb and learn to bear them.

For most of us, even in the most shocking loss, the full weight of our grief does not settle over us all at once. It is as if a hand holds something back. We encounter the first weight and stagger. Then regain our footing. Over a week's time, a month's, a year's—over years and years—we encounter the heaviness of loss again and again. In this way, we become stronger, accumulating strentgh slowly and becoming an ocean of strength, and the dark freight of grief—the longings, bittersweet memories, regrets, missed chances, lost dreams— all of it becomes bearable. The pains we have faced and borne have collected into greater strength than we knew. Gradually, an inner grace gives us the gift of an oceanic lightness, and we experience that buoyancy in spirit of which we never thought ourselves capable.

And yet growing in spirit is not automatic. Learning to have buoyancy of spirit begins with an act of simple recognition, a subtle but utterly indispensable change in perception. We start by acknowledging that there is a distinct and unending rhythm that runs through all of life.

Out of Grief . . . New Rhythm of Life

Life's pattern is ribboned with dark and light, gaining and losing. Furthermore, the pattern is more random than regular. We go for long periods of light and happiness, and suddenly meet the dark and difficult. Gaining this realistic perspective teaches us to accept both, and it gives us buoyancy to bear up well and with brightness in our spirits when darkness and loss come. Most of us do not come by a balanced perspective naturally. Nor, when we are faced with the darkness of pain and grief, do we really want to learn it. It may even seem "spiritual" to take the passive attitude that says, "What will be, will be . . .," or, "God's will be done." We want life to be all one way, or the other.

When a parent dies, we may sigh and say, "It was meant to be." That is fatalism. Or we may thoughtlessly, compulsively want to tidy things up quickly: an apartment, a file of papers, our emotions, and just "take care of business." That is materialism. Or we may say, "He/she died before his/her time. And it's not fair." And we carry anger and resentment. That is wounded judgmentalism. If we settle into these attitudes, which are automatic in every one of us, and do not work with our souls we will gain nothing.

For the sake of our souls we need a better plan. One that will allow us to explore our loss, and make gains in spirit. These gains do not come all at once but over time. And so we must become intentional as we approach our grief, recognizing it has presented us with inner tasks to do.

Working with Our Grief

How can we, in our grief, learn to have spiritual balance? How can we work with it to create vital buoyancy? Here are simple, strengthening practices we can develop.

Intentionality

Few of us take time to develop our inner beings. Rather, we let time take us. We rush around and tell ourselves we are too busy to think straight. This may actually be true, but it is not being responsive to our own needs. What we need is to become intentional about inner growth. We plan for vacations. We plan for our retirement income. We intend to have them and we invest time, energy, and money to get them. In a similar way, becoming intentional about growth in spirit is primary. Grief presents us with many pieces of unresolved, perhaps completely un-dealt-with, spiritual issues. Now is the time to become intentional by making the conscious choice to face and work with those issues.

Solitude

We may actually fear spending time alone. Many of us do. In the really long spaces of alone-time, demons of regret, self-accusation, and other painful voices emerge. When we are grieving the loss of a parent, a deep sense of abandonment may open up inside us. Now the voices in our lonely wilderness tell us, "You are alone. No one sees, or hears, or knows the depth of your loss." All our childhood terrors of vulnerability and death are stirred. It is this fear that tortures us most. Inner isolation is intense, as awful as any physical type of solitary confinement.

Most of us do not experience the intensity of our inner

fear of abandonment. We do not allow ourselves to. We sense the discomfort of its approach, and we turn on the television or radio, or rush to a phone, or go out for chit-chat over a cup of coffee. We fill our terror of alone-time with a crammed schedule of mostly meaningless "filler" activities. We have created this pattern over a lifetime, and it may become invisible to us. In grief, we can learn to be alone with ourselves without being terrified of being consumed by the terrors of abandonment. And even if our resistance to solitude is not that acute, we can learn how to use alone-time for our spiritual benefit.

We begin by setting a definite time to be alone. We can help to set the agenda by calling to mind pieces of unresolved business around our parent's death: a conversation we must have with a sibling; details of an estate to resolve; our own unsettled opinions about our parent; an unresolved conflict in our emotions.

Here, we enter in earnest into the "sifting the good/ sifting the bad" in order to come to a settled place. And so we begin to calm the inner ocean of shifting currents and find stability.

Quiet

"Only in quiet waters do things mirror themselves undistorted," said Hans Margolius. "Only in a quiet mind is adequate perception of the world."

Our parents were human and flawed, perhaps even riddled with contradictions. The unresolved conflicts they leave behind tend to become ours, part of our emotional inheritance. To follow Margolius' metaphor, the distortions that rippled the waters of our parents' souls are likely to distort ours, as well. The father who longs to love and be close to his child may be held back by a fear of making his child weak and unprepared for life in a tough world. His child inherits the conflict that voices itself this way: "I think my father loved me.

But if he did, why was he harsh so much of the time? Why couldn't he give me any of the affection I craved?"

When we allow ourselves to be alone and quiet, we find ourselves voicing the questions that, literally, form our life-quests. We touch the losses and lacks that drive us. At the same time, we can learn how to step back and observe these voices and the real influence they exert on us. That is, we can learn to distance ourselves. In this way, we begin to observe the workings of our inmost selves and build a self that is, finally, separate from the machinations our parents used to relate to and direct (manipulate?) us. Then it becomes possible to undo the burdensome ties to our parents by finding our own voices, and declaring our own, real, unquestioned, worth as separate individuals . . . and also determining our own passionately-felt direction in life. We learn to set a boundary between them and us.

When I had breast cancer, my mother really wanted to come and see me. I really wanted to be alone, especially right before the surgery. I wanted her to come at some later time, but I had only so much energy at the moment and wanted to steward it towards my husband and children. My mother would have upset the whole dynamic of our little household, and I knew it.

By taking the time to be alone and quiet, I was able to find the strength to tell my mother "no." She heard me, and accepted it. That gift of staying away was much more than she could have given me by coming. We were both able to self-differentiate, to create a space and time for the other.

Entering into quiet as adults, we often encounter the noise of left-over childhood quests. If we did not flex our muscles and declare independence from our parents when they were alive, it is time to do so now. By finding our own adult voices and values, we bring the disturbances of childhood that still weaken us, finally, to rest. In this way, we learn to see ourselves and the path we need to walk with our own eyes.

Bearing Weight and Becoming Light

Outside Reflection

Often the tasks of the inner life are difficult to perform alone. We have a hard time being honest while trying to sift the good from the bad. To say our parents did a bad thing feels too disloyal. ("What kind of child is disloyal? A terrible one!") We have a hard time differentiating their will for us, from our will for us. ("I really do want to be the successful business woman my mother wanted me to be, don't I? After all, even if I find no meaning or real joy in my work, I'm enjoying a good income and financial security, aren't I?") While our inner work begins with intention, solitude, and the work of quiet, we can all benefit from reflection from outside ourselves. In dealing with the issues that surface during grief, this is most especially necessary, because the event of death has a way of inducing our psyches to idealize a parent one way or the other, either as a perfect monster, or a perfect saint.

Often, too, the way our parents managed relationships with our sibling(s) has left those relationships in conflict. During grief, it is hard enough to face your own inner needs, let alone try to resolve relational tangles with a brother or sister. For these and other reasons I highly recommend you work with a professional counselor to help resolve issues encountered in grief.

Finding "Enough"

At the opening of this chapter, we enjoyed the words of a rich family blessing. We heard a father wish for his daughter to always have "enough." We heard a daughter express that her life, as it has been, is indeed "enough," a powerful statement of satisfaction and contentment with life.

In our grief we will encounter heaviness and even darkness. As we learn to work with the depths of our own souls, we begin to find the way to the blessing of "enough."

In the end, it is always the job of each individual to find his/her way to the land of enough. In the end, it is up to us to lay down the burdens too heavy to carry. And then to search inside ourselves, and know ourselves, and know what life and path and task is indeed ours to take up. Yes, we may encounter a special grief here, the grief that comes from recognizing that our parents' unfinished dreams and business will remain unfinished. But we need not remain children, yoked to our parents by cords of inner conflict and the desire to complete their lives and tasks for them. It is time to allow our parents to be the incomplete selves they were.

When we reach this point, we begin to experience an inner strength that might be called genuine authority. Perhaps all of our lives we have felt under the authority of inner compulsions, drives, and motives that did not seem true to who we were or what we wanted, as if we were dominated by some other force. And perhaps we were. Perhaps we were dominated and directed by needs, both conscious and unconscious, that were slid onto our shoulders by our parents, like a yoke. Genuine authority is the ability to have dominion ourselves, not the ability to control others. Letting go of our parents' burdens, as we let go of our parents, frees us to pursue uninterrupted intimacy with ourselves, our dreams and desires, the vitality of our own lives. We are no longer scattered within, trying to satisfy the demands of competing voices. We find the deeply satisfying life we have dreamed of having. And it is our own life. At last.

Artists of Our Own Lives

On November 18,1995, the great violin virtuoso, Itzhak Perlman, came on stage to give a concert at Avery Fisher Hall at Lincoln Center in New York City. Getting on stage is no small achievement for him. He was stricken with polio as a child, and so he has braces on both legs and walks with the aid of two crutches. The concert began, but just as he finished the first few bars, one of the strings on his violin broke. What now? Perlman waited a moment, closed his eyes and then signaled the conductor to begin again. The orchestra began, and he played from where he had left off. Despite the missing string, the amazing violinist played with passion, purity, and utter artistry, to the crowd's astonishment. When Perlman finished, there was an awesome silence in the hall. Followed by a thundering ovation. When the applause subsided at last, Perlman smiled and said in a calm voice, "You know, sometimes it is the artist's task to find out how much music you can still make with what you have left."

When a parent dies we have the opportunity, like Perlman, to discover what we can do with what we have left. That is when we find that we have indeed been given the blessing of enough.

Four

The Healing Work of Reconciliation

AFTER A BOUT WITH CANCER, John died peacefully in his sleep at the hospital. Because he learned the way to God through his own failures, John actually died at peace with his own soul and with God—certain that despite his huge failures he was going on to greater things.

John's wife, Carrie, had more of a struggle. She stuck with him through the seven-year prison sentence he served for murdering his own father. Now it hardly seemed fair that, after waiting faithfully for him all those years, she should be rewarded by having him taken from her. Nonetheless, Carrie's faith was also strong. As John reconciled with himself, he became a better husband to her, in many ways, even while in prison. Consequently, their relationship deepened spiritually even while he was behind bars. So she was able to reconcile with her loss, and bear it with extraordinary patience and grace.

Not so, John's son. He never quite forgave his father. At John's death, he focused on "all those wasted years" and experienced deep loss fed by anger and regret. With no sense of reconciliation, the loss was a bitter blow.

The way these three people responded to death is fascinating. One understood it as a passage from a lesser state to a greater state; another handled it with calmness and grace; one was stuck in bitter unforgiveness. I believe this scenario teaches us an important lesson: The way we learn to handle life is the way we will handle death, which is to say, we will be able to grieve well, to our own benefit, or we will grieve poorly, to our detriment.

Life Patterns

We are creatures of habit, mostly blind to our own interior patterns. Not surprisingly, the patterns we use to make our way through life are, in fact, the route we will take through grief. Many of our life-patterns keep us bound in resentment, unforgiveness, and keep us from moving on through the conflicts raised by grief to the greater maturity we desire. Unless we understand our patterns and alter them we can remain, like John's son, stuck in negativity.

Our patterns generally take one of two forms. That is to say, in life we are always, generally, moving toward one of two polarities. We are moving toward that which opens us to more of life, by which I mean emotional and spiritual life. Or we are moving toward that which closes us off and shuts us down, that is to say, we are moving toward death. That which moves us toward the embrace of life is courage, love, and the acceptance of the mixed-bag of our life and the people in them. That which moves us toward death is fear, hatred, and the rejection of lives and people and their screwy mixture. Love, the love of particular things in their mottled reality, is the axis around which spiritual wholeness turns. Love forms a whole. We want to receive love, and we want to know our love is received.

And so our movement through grief toward maturity comes down to this question: How will we relate to the mixed blessing and cursing we encounter in those to whom we want to give love and whose love we want to receive in return? Because "God is love" (1 John 4:8), when we speak of love at all—even our love for other human beings—God enters the picture.

God in the Picture

In previous chapters we considered the importance of dealing with relationship issues, the good and the bad, between us and the parents who left us through death. Sometimes when they have passed on we find ourselves "talking out" or raising old issues with them that were never raised in life. "Why didn't you love me more, and accept me for who I was?" "Why did you love me too much, in a smothering way?" But the fact is they are gone now, and we often find ourselves left to talk about them with God, the great Parent of us all.

Many of us move into a deepening relationship with God when our parents are gone. We find ourselves left alone with our relationship with God. Not surprising, we often find that our relationship with God may be similar in ways to the relationships we had with our parents. It is time to assess where we stand in this most central relationship of our whole lives. There are some who approach their relationship with God as if it were a "quick fix" for everything. "Oh, I'm sad my father is gone, but I have God." "Am I upset about losing my mother? Yes and no. I miss her, of course. But God will take care of me." We are the ones who, often, fail to deal with life's tough issues, hoping that "someone else" will step in and take care of them for us.

Others may see God as part of "the problem." "God never answered my prayers for my mother, why should I count on God now?" "My parents raised me to be strong and independent. I can't see the point in 'depending' on God. I depend on myself." We take an I-can-do-it-myself-thank-you attitude. Here again, we encounter deeply-ingrained patterns in our inner lives. For each of us, learning to relate well to God begins with recognizing the kind of God we have created in our heads based on our life experiences.

Beyond the examples above, some of us relate to a God who, according to our rules, is "supposed to" be there for us whenever needed, just as parents were "supposed to" be there for us when needed. We cannot stand discomfort and the insecure feeling of unsureness long enough to learn and grow through our struggles. Others of us have wanted both our parents and God to stay mostly out of our way. Perhaps we loathe inter-dependence because we are impatient with others' imperfections and processes. Or we may have created the kind of God who ponies-up with the power to cure, say, cancer . . . but only if we figure out the right buttering-up tactics, like saying "the right prayer" or "giving enough money to charity." This may be a reflection of God created by our sense that we have to "buy favor" with our parents. The secret of our success is manipulating for what we want.

Or we may have created a kind of God who delivers "justice NOW," possibly because we have lived with a strongly dominant parent whose decrees and judgments were swift and adamant. We prize decisiveness and a "take no prisoners" attitude, at the expense of fairness. We also have no patience, when in some situations waiting would be the best thing.

These "Gods" of our mental creation most often block our view of the true God.

Deep Calls to Deep

The One true God is, in the psalmist's metaphor, vast as an ocean. As "deep calls to deep" (Ps. 42:7), the true God is ever revealing new facets out of the eternal fathomlessness of divine Being.

Once we have seen the God of our own imaginations, we can acknowledge that we have relied on the shallow strengths of a false god upon whom we have called to take care of the surface needs of life. The deeper needs we have not trusted to God. The deeper aspects of character we have not allowed to be touched by God. And so the God with whom we have related has been seriously limited, and our relationship with the divine seriously flawed.

We begin a new and more mature relationship with God when we can acknowledge our need to meet the true God who comes to us, with hand outstretched, eager to reveal new facets of personality we have never yet been open enough to encounter. This God, the One with many depths and dimensions, the One who is the source of all life, is the God who wants to be in a right and life-giving relationship with us. Perhaps we think we are not "ready" for a growing, deepening relationship with God. The question then is: What will make us ready?

God Is Stuck

God is stuck in a pattern. Call it a divine rut. No matter what we do, whether we move toward love or toward bitter anger, God stays in the relationship with us. God calls that relationship a covenant. Many of us, today, have little idea what this word means. We think "contract," a basis of relating that is founded in a coldly calculated legal agreement, binding each party to the performance of certain duties and obligations. Perform; be rewarded. Fail to perform; the contract is broken and you are open to prosecution and making redress.

Covenant is founded in a relationship. A covenant is a holy relationship. Covenant is different from contract. God did not decide to love us and make a contract that lists the terms of love. Rather, because God loves us he is stuck, as it were, in a covenant of love with us. God's hopeless I-am-stuck-because-of-love resounds in the words of Ruth, so often quoted at weddings: "Don't urge me to leave you or turn back from you. Where you go I will go . . . " (Ruth 1:16). In a contractual relationship we may have to press our case, point to clauses, argue for what is ours "by right," or because we have "performed our part and now your part is due." In a covenant there is none of that. No this-for-that spirit exists. God, by a free act, stays close to us whether or not we stay close to God.

To grasp this irrevocable commitment on God's part is to experience the spiritual lights coming on, what some call "spiritual enlightenment" and what others call "salvation," the beginning of the soul's movement from its fractured state of immaturity toward wholeness. Recognizing the true God who loves us with total abandon becomes our path to the interior unity that is spiritual maturity. Only in an atmosphere of utter trust can we open ourselves to anyone, even God. And yet, God has abandoned himself to us, trusting that as he remains in a covenant of love with us we will open our deepest beings to him. Will we trust this God, and open our souls, and continue to grow?

Hold on a Minute . . .

Some of us are jaded by life and its misfortunes. Perhaps we trusted God at one time. But bad things have happened. Perhaps we prayed for our parents not to die, or at least to escape an uncomfortable or untimely death. But what we greatly feared, what we did not want to happen, happened.

Awhile back, attending a conference on Spirituality and the Arts in New York City, I had lunch with Heather, a young woman who is now twenty-eight, an editor with *Time* magazine, and whose life has been marked by tragedy. Heather had been my best confirmation student, with a true connection to God through faith. Ironically, the year Heather was confirmed, at fourteen, her brother was in a minor car accident, which caused his spleen to split. He lived just four hours after the crash. He was only eight. What a huge betrayal it seemed to Heather: she had just affirmed her faith in a God of love, and such a small quirk of events claimed the life of her little brother. Initially, Heather could not believe in God any more, and she turned her back on faith.

But that was not the end of the story. Something in Heather kept urging her to say "yes" to life. Not necessarily "yes" to God, but to life. To her surprise, where she found life she also found God. She "left God behind," only to find God waiting on the path ahead of her. One small step at a time, she returned to a relationship with God. Today, many questions remain for Heather about God and faith. Yet it is as if, through inner urgings to keep embracing life, God is saying to her, "I want us to be reconciled. Despite the 'evidence' you're holding onto—your brother's tragic death—I never left you."

In the final analysis, what keeps most of us from reconciling with God is the mixed-bag of life. We want a guarantee that, if we are going to let God into the picture he must offer a guarantee, promising us no overwhelming difficulties, and especially, no losses. We want contract, not covenant.

When a couple weds, there is absolutely no guarantee that one can keep the other from harm and loss. For reasons unknown to us, the God who is head-over-heels stuck in a covenant of love with us offers no guarantees that bad things will not happen, and no explanations as to why they do. What God the unfathomable and limitless One says is, "I will be with you always" (Matt. 28:20). We are the ones who want a performance contract: God offers relationship. We will offer God our closeness, if he performs. He offers never to leave our side no matter what. We say, "Unless you do as I say I will hold your failures against you." He says, "I remember your sins and failures no more" (Isa. 43:25).

This is the God who has bound himself to us by a covenant. God's pattern is to remain constant, when all around us is changing and inconstant, and even when we ourselves are changeable toward him. This is God's pattern. God cannot help himself.

The Healing Work of Reconciliation

What I want to point out here, though, is the pattern that brought Heather through grief to a maturing perspective on life. She did not have to keep saying "yes" to God. She had only to say "yes" to life. Many of us refuse to meet life on the terms in which it comes to us. We create patterns of resistance, holding out for what we want. And so we close off our spirits to change and growth. When we say "yes" to life as it comes to us—with its mixture of gains and losses, tragedies and joyful wonders—we open the door to spiritual maturity. This will ever be so, because we are, at the same time, opening ourselves to the God who is life.

Life without Guarantees—
Life without Limits

Somewhere deep inside each one of us there exists a child who wants iron-clad guarantees. We want life never to disappoint or hurt us. We want our parents never to leave us. And above all, we want God to be the Great Guarantor. We want a God who steps back and allows us to set up the world just the way we want it, and then says, "Now that you've got things arranged just the way you like them, I'll do my best to keep them that way." The true God offers no such promises or guarantees. But at the same time he promises to be with us in this life without limits. "Neither death nor life," says the Apostle Paul, "is able to separate us from the love of God . . ." (Rom. 8:38). As we open ourselves to this great love of God, we begin to find life beyond the seemingly hard, cold limits of death.

In order to move on through grief to maturity in spirit, we are asked to recognize that we have come to our limits of human understanding. Only God can reconcile our great longing to embrace life with the fact of death. In grief we come face to face with what the undeveloped soul may call "the senselessness of it all." In truth we are coming face to face with great patterns of light and dark, gaining and losing—

with contradictions and ambiguities—that cannot be made sense of by the small, human mind. They can only be perceived, felt, intuited by the spirit that is reconciled and in relationship with God. Only when we stop focusing solely on our patterns of losses, and say "yes," opening to what can be added to us, can we mature in spirit and detect the first outlines of "a greater sense about things."

Death Is a Door

"Death is a door," says a poet. Not just to eternity, but to becoming present to the God who is always present to us. Death can lead to spiritual enlightenment, our salvation, because it gets our complete attention.

Stephen Heifitz has written a Nobel Laureate-winning symphony, in which he uses drums to announce, every 3.6 seconds, that someone is dying from hunger. Listen with just your head and you can hear the drums beating like the heart of the world with its grievous losses. But listen with your spirit and you hear the heartbeat of God, coming to us in our many griefs, beckoning us to be reconciled with him in order that we may gain the wisdom to be reconciled with our losses.

The world will persist in sending us suffering and death. And God, for his part, will persist in coming to us, reaching toward us, loving us. He will persist in reaffirming the covenant he wishes there to be between us, whispering, "I will be your God and you will be my people."

In times of grief, responding to that whisper will help us reconcile with the life and love we have lost, and move us on to the deepening life that can be ours.

Five

Beyond Indifference

KAREN'S FATHER DIED ON Saturday. With a few phone calls, she made all the arrangements for his funeral, which would be on Tuesday. Monday she went to work as usual, and bowled with friends that evening. The news of her father's death all but disappeared into the relaxed fun of an evening with people whose company she enjoyed.

At first, Karen thought nothing about the blandness of her reaction. Her relationship with her father had become distant long ago. At the time of his death, she had not seen him for months and months. After years of little contact, she learned he had been moved into a nursing home several hours from her. But since he no longer even recognized her, she had given up visiting him, except on an occasional holiday. As far as the rest of her family, nothing was offered to her or expected from her.

The funeral was on Tuesday morning. The service itself was sad, almost pathetic, attended only by two people from the funeral home, Karen and her secretary, a friend, and an old aunt who was informed by the nursing home that her brother-in-law had died. Karen's mother was dead, and Karen had called no one because she had been out of her parents' lives so long she did not know anyone to call. The graveside prayers and committal service were followed by settling-up financial obligations with the director that afternoon. Tuesday evening, Karen went out to a movie she had been wanting to see.

On Wednesday, however, driving to work, Karen knew something was odd here. On one level, it was back to the main road of life as usual. But something else was going on at another level, and she could not quite put her finger on it, until a co-worker said, timidly, "Gee, you're either handling the death of your father extremely well for some reason, or you are indifferent. I can't tell which."

Sitting at her desk awhile later, Karen suddenly dropped her pen, feeling as if someone had punched the wind out of her. A wave of anguish came up from inside. It was the huge and unpleasant sense of discrepancy she felt. With the thought, "When your parent dies you should feel something," the nature of her grief struck home.

That day, she understood that grief can come, even in the wake of indifference.

When It Is Too Risky to Care

Karen continued to trouble over her lack of response to her father's death. Over and over, she thought, "Both parents are dead now. My father just died, he's gone and I'll never have a relationship with him. So why don't I care?" Beneath that question, of course, was another: "What kind of daughter, what kind of a human being, doesn't care that her father has just died?"

When it comes to the death of a parent, and we experience indifference, it does not mean that we lack the human capacity to care or love. Usually, it is an emotional signpost pointing back to a time when we made the decision not to care. In Karen's case, her parents had a long history of neglect. They had been self-involved, caught up in their own inner and outer lives. Not only had they failed to adequately nurture, care for, or protect her when needed, they showed no interest in her achievements when she left home to create a life of her own. Any attempts to share her life with them, in hopes of some show of real interest and enthusiasm, were met with nothing in response.

The truth is, when a relationship with a parent has been shut down, because of his/her neglect, the most common response at his/her death is indifference. In Spanish, we say about indifference, *No vale la pena* (It's not worth the pain.). At a deep level we have calculated a "cost-benefits analysis," and we do not see benefit in caring. In Karen's case, her family taught her to be distant, to keep herself emotionally and mentally disconnected.

Others, like Jeff, become indifferent because they lacked freedom in the relationship with their parents. Jeff's father was domineering and forceful, always insisting he knew what was best for Jeff and belittling Jeff's opinions and choices. For Jeff, connection came to mean "bound." Eventually, he withdrew further and further from his dad, and the more irate his father became the more Jeff disconnected and became indifferent. "What he thinks does not make a bit of difference to me. What I want doesn't matter to him, so let's see how he likes it if I don't give a damn about him. Sure , I'd like to have a father to be close to, but I can't trust the one I have." For Karen and Jeff both, it was too risky to care.

Oddly enough, our choice to be indifferent toward a parent does not mean we have disconnected. Benumbed though we may be, there remains an emotional nerve-link, a bond, that continues to tether us to this human source of our very being. Yes, the emotional nerve-channels may be devoid of warm sensations such as love or even liking. Nonetheless, we remain connected to our parents, as Karen discovered.

Pragmatically speaking, when we feel indifferent at losing a parent it is most often a conditioned response. It is normal, given the fact that we have experienced indifference toward us.

Karen had been trained a long time ago that caring got her nowhere. Beyond the basic sense of familial obligation, she gave up wanting warm feelings to be stirred by having her parent care about her, and her warm feelings of caring about her father had long ago cooled, as well. On the death of her father, she acted authentically out of her experience and heart. She felt no deep distress and did not pretend to, and yet she honored her father by managing the details of his final memorial service.

Eventually, Karen was able to come to terms with the "oddness" she sensed, and to understand that it was rooted in her parents' odd choice to have a child but to remain emotionally aloof from her. They had never really honored her by showing much care in any way. And in that light, her final efforts in setting up memorial services was a sign of as much honor as she could offer. Still, Karen's indifference, most recently, at the loss of her father, continues to trouble her.

The Danger of Indifference

Indifference is not neutral. Feelings of indifference toward people who are otherwise close to us biologically do have consequences. At some point, indifference takes on an aggressive nature and spreads. Inwardly, silently, indifference creates attitudes of disconnectedness, and this in turn creates more indifference. The less and less we know, the less and less we care. Deepening indifference and disconnectedness form patterns in the soul. They can begin to permeate all our relationships. Not only does indifference distance and "protect" us from emotional pain, it disconnects us from the security, playfulness, wisdom, and the connections we gain from others. In our wariness about becoming too attached to anyone, we close down into smaller and tighter circles of affiliation. When a pattern of indifference and disconnection is deep enough, we may no longer recognize the benefit of friendly or intimate relationships. Love, because it is too great and risky an inner distance to travel, because it is often a relationship between opposites who are fascinatedly attracted to each other, may become out of the question. And so we may tell ourselves that our parents' indifference taught us not to risk loving. But life is risk and love is risk. And at the base of it all, down in our unconscious souls, a pattern of indifference—ours—is eroding and gradually undermining our ability to love.

Love is the opposite of indifference. Love contains the ability to embrace difference. The distinct differences of the ones we love fascinate and draw us to them. Riddled with flaws and perfections and much that is in process, they nonetheless matter to us. Love is when a person matters to us and we matter to them. The danger of indifference is that its cool voice will always encourage us to keep loose connections, even to those we deeply want to love, to be ready to run at the first sign that all is not perfectly well. But life and everyone in it is imperfect. Indifference, left unchecked, erodes not only love but life, as well.

Back to the Beginning

Yes, parents are the ones who help create the patterns that give character to our souls. With their love or lack of love, with their concern and enthusiasm or indifference, they show us the pathways down which we can journey into life. For most of us, the relationship with our parents ebbs and flows, assumes greater and lesser importance, may be punctuated by times of less and more contact. But the relationship patterns begun here go deep and run through our whole lives.

Some parents have a profound effect. Daughters go off to imitate their father's ambitious approach to all of life, from hobbies to health, and from fitness to work. Sons adopt their mother's gentle and wise use of intelligence, not coldly picking things and people apart, but striving compassionately to understand. When a business decision must be made, a son may think, "What would Dad do?" When a daughter finds herself nearly overwhelmed with the challenges of work, children, and a home, she may think, "How did Mom handle all of this with such grace and efficiency?"

There are less-important patterns created, affecting the way we approach the simpler things of life. A man may find himself folding dish towels the way his mother used to do it. A woman may find that she keeps to a rigorous schedule of auto maintenance, just like her dad did.

Sometimes, of course, those patterns are negative. Don's family had a long history of cutting people off, after an offense or serious disagreement. His mother's sister lived right next door during his growing-up years, and sometimes they would not speak to each other, literally, for months and months. Once they went more than three years without speaking, though in the end, no one could even remember the offense that caused the severing of relations. Eventually, Don's mother and her sister had a final falling-out and stopped speaking altogether. When he asked his mother if it bothered her to have lost her sister, she just shrugged indifferently. "Sister . . . that word doesn't mean anything to me," she said.

"I actually hated this about my family," says Don. "I thought it was stupid and childish. But after three years of marriage, my relationship with my wife was coming apart. It startled me when she pointed out that every time she hurt me—usually not meaning to—I refused to be honest and deal with it. Instead, I just shut down and would not talk about it. "What scared me was this. When my wife pointed out my pattern I realized that inwardly I'd been growing indifferent. I'd even said, secretly, 'Go ahead and leave. What would I care?' That family pattern of cutting people off had been passed on to me, and now it was at the root of our marriage problems."

We do repeat the patterns we learn as children, including

patterns that connect us to others, as well as patterns that disconnect us. These can remain with us throughout our whole lives, affecting every relationship we enter into.

Blocking the Truth

Sometimes we do not recognize our own indifference. As one woman put it, after her mother's death, "I'm not indifferent, I just don't care." The fact is, we can come up with different methods of closing down, refusing to see the truth, and stopping our own growth. As the old saying goes, "There is none so blind as he that will not see." Some of us simply do not want to face our indifference. Underneath, a voice is saying, "What kind of son or daughter is indifferent to their parent's death?" The answer implied of course, is "a bad one," one who has defects that makes him or her unnatural, not human. Because we do not want to see ourselves as "heartless" we refuse to look at our indifference and call it what it is.

Adopting religious sympathies can also cover over our lack of feelings at the death of a parent. Indifference, not faith, can hide itself in expressions like, "I think God took them for a better purpose," or "Praise God, she's in heaven now." Personally, I must say I dislike the practice of using God and his "higher purposes" as a reason to by-pass the anguish and inner struggle of grief. Sometimes those who do so come up with sugar-candy explanations that, one can only suppose, are meant to comfort. "God needed your Mom in heaven." ("But I need her here.") "God loved your Dad and took him home." ("God has plenty of people to love. I had only one father.") Well-intended as these treacly sentiments may be, all they do in fact is to create the image of a God who is, at best, indifferent to our loss and pain or, at worst, a cosmic sadist. Whatever our methods of creating indifference, these are attempts to pack away grief, ways to force ourselves not to look. Perhaps indifference is really our attempt to stem the flood of a lifetime's worth of grief, a way to keep ourselves from feeling the bereftness and abandonment this parent has always made us feel.

Please hear me clearly: Because we are human, with complex mental (and therefore, emotional) capabilities, we are able to feel more than one feeling at a time. We say, all the time, "I have mixed feelings about such and such."

This being true, it seems more realistic, and quite likely truer and more healthy to say, "My father is dead. He never showed me he cared . . . and so it's hard to really care about his passing. So I'm not sure why I do care." If we are people of great faith we might say, "I believe that in the providence of God there is a reason why she was taken from this earth at this time. She's not sick or suffering any more, and that is a good thing. But there is unfinished inner business for me. Her lack of caring left deficits in my life, and I need to find out what to do about that." Finding our way through grief, for many of us, will mean finding our way through the forest of mixed feelings. If we take on this important work, it will move us on to greater maturity in spirit.

Growing Is All about Connection

So we return to the issue of indifference and our ability to create healthy, lasting emotional connections. When we have experienced weakened ties in that most primary of relationships, with our parents, there can exist a substrata of indifference. Beneath all our other relationships, even those we claim are important to us, lies a wary aloofness, a readiness to cut ties and quench warm feelings, at the first sign that the other party is acting cool and uncaring. We may be telling ourselves, "It's not worth it to care about other people. They never really care about me."

But a life worth living is all about connections. We must guard against indulging ourselves in indifference, that is, in the attempt to neglect-to-death relationships in which we are bruised by neglect or by aggression. We will never escape these relational bumps, as long as we live on this planet.

Our goal, instead, should be to build health and goodness in all our connections. The long term injury to our self and, quite likely, our own children, if we let indifference weaken our relationships, is far too great. We need the inner strength that comes from sharing long histories, filled with ups and downs and testings and provings, in our relationships with other people. We need to love and be loved, long, and for all that we are and are not. We need to learn the flexibility that takes the good with the bad; strengths with weaknesses; and faults, failings, and lacks along with the gifts. We also need to know we make a difference in someone's life and grow close with that someone who makes a difference in ours.

When grief brings us face-to-face with our patterns of indifference, how can we counter those life-impairing effects? How can reverse our tendency to disconnect, and deepen and mature in our human connections?

Reconnecting

Our ability to change begins when we take a long hard look at our attitudes, those inner postures that incline us toward indifference and disconnection. Attitudes are the fuel for our thoughts and actions. Perhaps the attitude that has grown in us is that we do not need anyone. Or that someone needs to really prove they are interested in us, before we will reach back and show interest in him or her. It may be that we keep relationships cool and noncommittal "just in case" we detect a problem and need to bail-out fast. There are dozens of ways to describe the attitudes that fuel indifference. It may be that we need the help of a counselor, therapist, or spiritual director to see our attitudes. Even so, we are the ones who must choose the posture we will take toward life and love, and we alone can choose whether or not to incline ourselves toward the building of long-term relationships that are deepening in intimacy, emotional, and spiritual good health. The move toward connection is a move toward greater maturity.

Even so, it is a move we are wise to take in small steps.

There is no need to feel that we should be opening all sectors of our outer and inner lives to someone quickly in order to make up for the relationship we have been missing with our parents. That intense approach may burn us and the other person out. Taking our time, opening ourselves when it is appropriate, this is key to building connections. We can also help ourselves by staying open to the idea of finding surrogate parents. Our need for parenting—that is, for someone with a more-experienced and wiser perspective who has permission to speak honestly—never ends. We do not have to look for "the perfect" replacement; in fact, if we idealize what "the perfect" father or mother would be like and set out to find that in one individual we will be looking the rest of our lives. Far better to look for the qualities we need in a number of surrogates, a sort of life counsel, like business mentors, people with parenting and grandparenting experience, those who have lived through the ups and downs of marriage, or others who have faced the highs and lows of living. If we take this broader approach, candidates are everywhere. We can find them in church groups, in nursing homes, sometimes in social or civic clubs.

As we move to change indifference into living connections we help ourselves not only by learning to be open about ourselves, but by learning to listen and care about others. In particular, those we look to for their parental qualities also need us to listen to them. They are moving ahead of us on life's path, facing issues of aging, health, financial preparedness, retirement, and more. They are on the front-edge of their own life's path, encountering emotions, needs, and conditions never experienced before. Yes, we need them; but we cannot forget that we are needed, too.

In fact, building mutuality into a relationship is an important mark of maturity. It tells us we are moving on from indifference, and that we are deepening in spirit.

The Road to Deepening Relationships

When you have spent a long time, maybe most of a lifetime, learning to be indifferent it is tempting to listen to the voice that says, "What if my choice is not to care?" Obviously we have alternatives. The question is: "Which alternatives are healthy?" We may choose to stay disconnected, because connecting is so tricky or so foreign. We may not know how, really, though we are adults, to connect with others in healthy ways. We hold on too loosely, because we fear we will come to care too much, and lose friends because it seems we do not care enough. We clutch too tightly, out of fear we will be left alone and disappointed again, and drive people away with our attempts to dominate and control.

When I think of learning how to build healthy connectedness, the word "tethered" comes to mind. To be "tethered" is to be lightly, loosely tied-to. It is not "roped to"; it is not "clutching in a strangle-hold." Connecting with others means relating with the firm strength of a tether, held lightly, loosely in the hand. It may be one of the profoundest acts of healing, when familial ties have been cut or allowed to atrophy, to reconnect with our "sense of family." The impulse may be to pull even further away from family and forget that we have a heritage and history. But to do so is to cut ourselves off further from a sort of tribal rootedness that can give us great stability and sense of well-being, a sense of "knowing who we are and where we have come from."

Some people restore familial ties by making plans to visit with other family members. After the death of his father, Ken chose to travel across country and locate his father's brother. The two men had been estranged, but Ken found a warm welcome. "I know you and I don't know each other very well, but you are my brother's son, and I want you to count on me and call me whenever you need anything," Ken's uncle said. Slowly, Ken is finding a measure of closeness and trust with his uncle that he never had with his own father. Others find reconnection in working to reestablish the family hierarchy. Sometimes a parent has become the "hub" of family activity. After their death it is necessary to create a new center, a place to gather for holidays, a sort of council to make family decisions.

Give Yourself Time

It takes many years for a stream of water to carve a fissure in the ground. If the stream dries up, it takes many years for the gash to close and return to solid ground on which it is safe to walk. When our souls have been marred by indifference, we need to be as patient as we are brave, as we allow healing to take place. When a parent's death has left us full of numb indifference, we need not stay stuck there. The good news is, with care and patience we can reclaim ability to connect deeply with others. If we take up the challenge, we may find what we have been hungering for, mutually-caring relationships that make life rich and full.

Six

The Work
of Separation

An acquaintance recently gave me a poem she wrote about her last moments with her mother. I found myself deeply moved.

Reading Aloud to My Mother

After dinner on those last days
we hoped would linger until the thinning moon rose
into the numb sky,

I sat beside her bed
and read from the novel she'd begun
months before on her own.

At first the words wouldn't leave
the page. Then, like crows nibbling invisible debris
on the uneven horizon, longing
to grow invisible themselves,
they unpredictably
lifted all at once above it
and pushed across the darkening sky—
a tribe of inky letters
on a page that itself was slowly growing black

until the words, there or not, were mute
as the new moon that in a few days
would rise and fall again in the black sky
and I would be there and watching
and would not see it.

—Andrea Hollander Budy

In Andrea's words, she had had holy time with her mother—
the woman she loved most in the whole world—before
losing her to this thing we call death. And this poem gives
voice to the muted grief she could not speak of through
choking tears. Not long after, Richard Sparrow wrote a
prayer based on her poem.

Thank you, God, for holy time
when clock gives way to heart
and minutes are simply spent
in ways too deep for expression.

Thank you, God, for first times
when rocking one so small
creates a bond where you
weave our lives for lifetime . . .
and for those middle times
when looking at another we know
there never was a time
when we didn't know each other

and for those ending times
when memories are so rich
that tears are more from
grateful memories than from loss.

Thank you, God, for holy times
that sometimes we miss
but more often cause us to stop

and wonder as grace fills our cup
to running-over full.

—Richard Sparrow

The connection between these two women seems holy. Andrea was known by her mother, and she knew her mother. At the time of her mother's death they were vividly alive to each other. It is no wonder her words of grief—those black crows on a black horizon—stuck in her throat. They had a love for each other that ran deep. Perhaps the depth of their bond was the reason Andrea felt stuck for months and months after her mother's death, unable to move on toward the beckoning and brighter horizon of her own future.

The last memory Golda had of her mother was of an angry old woman yelling that she had placed a pillow the wrong way beneath her head. The last words her mother left her with were, "Go away, Golda. Just go away." Golda's mother had spent a lifetime battering her daughter with destructive and rejecting comments. The woman was a veritable iceberg. In fact, Golda was not only relieved when her mother died she was, to use her words, "almost ecstatic." She felt a kind of relief she had not known throughout the forty-six years of her life. She had lived alone with her mother after her father died suddenly of a heart attack when she was ten. Finally there was no one to complain to her or about her.

Quite obviously, Golda's response to her mother's death was exactly the opposite of Andrea's. At least on the surface. Like Andrea, though, Golda soon found herself stuck and unable to move on with her own life. What was happening? Why could neither woman freely move on with her life?

Separation

The death of a parent is something that happens to you. It is an outer event. You sit there passively, and it flows over you.

Clearly, someone was there; now he/she is gone. As we have seen in previous chapters, however, so many energies are at work inside—thoughts, moods, feelings, impulses to resolve the matters of tangible property and personal business—each one needing to be directed. In Andrea's case, and Golda's too, each woman was stuck because she needed to know clearly what to do with the remnants of the particular bond remaining with her mother, holding her in a static position. Inwardly, the issues of final separation remained. The parent was gone, but not the connection. For these two women, of course, the connection was different.

In Golda's case, the residual "bond" was spun, like a spider's web, of negative filaments, of insults and criticisms and rejections. In Andrea's case, the bond was composed and beautiful, like a flowerbed, with living and intermingled colors of support given and received, mutual respect, loving words, and caring actions.

The one thing that both situations had in common was this: Each woman now needed to move on by stepping into a new identity that was totally free of her parent's influence. It was time to separate, and emerge from that greater, enveloping co-identity, into an identity all her own.

Separation-from-and-emergence-to is one of the deeper works of grief, reaching to the roots of our being. Separation is the beginning, and emergence is the result, of a powerful process that propels us on and leads us to possession of a solid experience of our own adulthood, a self-possession we may have dimly imagined.

For Golda, separation could only begin as she learned how to end the relationship with her mother. It would mean finding her own way of putting an end to the bad memories and negative voices, the self-disgust and disdain, that clung, like thick webs, in her soul. Only if she cleared the dark corners of their clots could she be free to encounter the unexplored and undeveloped rooms of her own soul and, eventually, become the owner of the house of her own soul. Andrea's journey of separation and emergence would require similar work. But in her case, it would be more careful and painstaking, like separating out varieties of flowers in a bed where wonderful things grew, but that had invaded each other's space. Their relationship, beautiful as it was, had become like a neglected garden, the borders of one pretty variety infiltrating the alloted space of another. Like Golda, Andrea also needed to create interior space so that the parts of herself that had yet to emerge could bud and blossom.

Relief

It is one of the more shocking and guilt-inducing experiences of grief to realize that you are, either a little or a great deal, glad your parent is gone. Few people understand, much less know what to do with, the relief and growing sense of freedom they feel. When Golda and Andrea were honest, they could admit that they felt a measure of relief. Though Golda's connection to her mother was negative, and Andrea's was tremendously positive, ironically, both these women had been kept from emerging into a fully-realized adult identity. Eventually, it dawned on both of them that a new future, based on a solo identity, beckoned invitingly. Now both faced the same task, the work of building her own life.

Some say it is never too late to have a happy childhood, but that is only true if we can find a way to put the parent away, to store him or her in a safe place so we can get on with life. For Andrea, the task of separation was much like the labor most gardeners face come August. We have to face overgrown gardens, and redefine the limits for the flowers that have gone rampant, encroaching on each other's territory. It is not that what is there is ugly or malignant, but unless every flower is made to honor its own boundaries nothing can be seen in its full glory. If we do not separate out the white daisies from the gold, trumpeting day lilies, neither will bloom well next year. They will eventually crowd out each other's life.

Andrea's working through grief required her to think of "separating out" her life from her mother's. "What do I really love? And what did I merely like just because Mom liked it and I loved her?" Because our life is fed by our passions, this was the same as asking, "What was Mom's life? What was shared? And what is my life?" Slowly, as Andrea worked through this separation process, she was able to let go of her mother a little at a time. That pastime was something her mother had loved, and now that her mother was gone it was time for it to rest, as well. This was something Andrea had longed to try, but had not allowed herself time to do. Now was her time. In this way, a new identity—and a new life—found room to emerge and thrive.

When we have a warm and close relationship with our parents, it is easy to keep on living with them and to stunt our own growth, even after they are gone. Andrea was able to avoid that trap, and now has her own life, with a forward momentum of her own.

Golda had her own inner work to do. For her it began, as you might guess, with "cleaning out the spider webs" of negative, self-debasing thoughts and memories. For this, she required the help of a counselor because her mother's assessment of her ("You're so stupid") seemed to be her own, as well. But cleaning out the toxic residue left by her mother was only a piece of the work. Golda found she needed to go way back in her life to find a time when there were positive words and affirming experiences. That is to say, she needed to find the good and wholesome roots of her own being. For her, this meant returning in memory to the time before she was ten. With her father, there had been golden moments, a gallery of good memories she could call upon without risk, because they were warm and affirming of her. As Golda bravely did this double-edged work, a wonderful sense of emergence began to replace the "stuck and going nowhere" feeling that had held her back. She was able both to cut away the webs of her mother's negativity and see herself as a person of value. Even if her mother had not valued her much, she could value herself - her likes and dislikes, her whims and her dreams. After many, many years, Golda felt free just to be.

Hard Choices

Roger's experience, after losing his mother, stands in contrast to Andrea's and Golda's.

Roger's mother left him a fine, small business—a little workshop that made flags. Since she was every bit the matriarch at home and at the shop, her strong will, and opinions, and business decisions governed almost every part of Roger's life. And though he never much liked the flag business, he did like being with his mother. She was a lot of fun. After her death, Roger had opportunities to sell the flag business. He very much wanted to because it was dull. And yet he could not bring himself to let it go. To this day, Roger feels thwarted and unhappy. By holding on to the business, Roger kept himself from making other choices that would have allowed his own personality and life to emerge. In order to stay close to fond memories and the association with his mother, he stunted his own growth into maturity.

There is nothing morally wrong with Roger's choice, though it clearly suppresses his own spirit. Still, it is his choice. What is most sad, perhaps, is that his mother still dominates both his inner and outer life. "Mother," says Roger, "would never sell the flag business." And so, Roger's mother's life continues to stand in place of his own.

Finding the Gift

Archibald MacLeish said about his wife: "The greatest and richest good—my own life to live in—this she has given me."

This gift, our own life to live in, is what we need most, especially from our parents. It is the gift Golda and Andrea and Roger all needed. It is the singular gift given to us by God alone. And it is the one our parents, in their humanness, most often fail to respect. In many ways, our parents bind us to themselves and to their lives. In many ways, either because we do not want to face the world on our own, or because the lives handed to us are comfortable and convenient , we bind ourselves to our parents and the paths they have chosen. Many of us have hardly even begun the process of separating from them in any conscious and beneficial way. Is it any wonder the path ahead becomes unclear for many of us and we feel, we say, "lost." And so we are left at the time of their deaths to go about the work of finding the gift that is our own individual life.

Separating our lives from our parents' lives is delicate work, requiring great patience and care. We need to know what to preserve and what to let go, and this is exactly what we do not know for sure. Here, I am reminded of my own efforts to work around a delicate thing I discovered in my garden one fall day, a spider's web. Earlier I used the image of a web, in speaking of Golda and her mother, in a totally negative sense. The light glancing down into my garden, slant and yellow-gold, revealed a web of great beauty. In fact, it was the angle of the light at this time of day, 7 a.m., that allowed me to see the web at all. I had come out to clean, and weed, and fix up the garden. But the brilliance of light on fine-spun filament was arresting. The web was complicated and utterly perfect: a masterpiece. I studied it, amazed at the natural artistry.

Very consciously, I made the decision to avoid the web at all costs, cordoning off in my mind the area where it hung the way you would rope off a rare, museum piece. Happily, I went about my work. And in no time I was absorbed with pulling weeds and wiping sweat from my brow, reaching up at one point to brush not only moisture but some sort of sticky netting from my cheek. And in a shock it hit me. The web! Unintentionally, I had blundered into the very thing I had vowed to protect and preserve. Not knowing what I was doing, I had robbed the world of this delicate treasure.

We will not always choose perfectly, as we decide which of the things that connect us to our parents we need to keep and which we need to let go, if we are going to emerge more completely ourselves. Monica had felt tremendously stifled in the small eastern town where she settled "to stay close to my Dad." When he passed away after a long illness, she lost no time, selling both her and her father's homes and moving to the west coast, where she had dreamed of living for years. In only months, however, she felt rootless and totally out of place. With the clarity of hindsight, she now saw the golden glint of value in so many things about her life back in that small eastern town. Packing again, she moved back.

Though Monica desperately wanted to purchase her father's home again, the new owner was not interested in selling. "I wish I'd never sold Dad's place. That's a decision I really regret. I guess I had to run away from home," she says, thoughtfully, "to see what I really had at home. Now I know a lot more about who I am and where I belong." For Monica, as for all of us, the process of separating in order to emerge may lead us through imperfect choices. But it will also lead us to wisdom and insight, and to a sense of ownership about our lives and the choices we are making.

Maturity . . . and New Birth

If we are going to separate in order to emerge, we do well to accept this truth, difficult to grasp, yet freeing: Maturity is about owning our choices and our lives. Letting go of a parent who has died is not just about loss. We are making our way to a life, an identity, that is new. This, it seems, is the order of things: Something old must die if something new is to emerge.

In grief, as in all life's great passages, we die to something

The Work of Separation

81

and are reborn to something else. If we refuse to go through life's passages, we will remain stuck where we were. Knotted. Paralyzed. Unable to move on. We remain afraid of our own lives, afraid of our own dreams. We will, if we remain afraid, wind up stuck in a largely unlived life. Those who do set out to find the adult identity that is truly their own find the pearl of great price, the gift of a life that is theirs alone to live. And they experience something else, a sense of being accompanied by the Divine. And why not? Is not the pathway they are following laid out by God? Why would he not be found along its rugged way? As one hymnist has written, "I was there to hear your borning cry. I'll be there when you are old." (John Ylvisaker)

Let us, in our grief, remember that up ahead there awaits a new birth out of this death, a newer, truer self than we have yet seen. And let us move on toward this goal with a confidence born of faith.

Seven

Death Is a Door

MANY POETS DESCRIBE DEATH as a door or a gate—an opening, not a closing. My friend Sonya recently had an arresting experience that would seem to prove there is truth in the poet's sentiment. Not long ago, Sonya's mother died, peacefully and at home with her children surrounding her, just the way she hoped to die. At the moment of her death, Sonya was startled to see a white silky form, like a graceful scarf, unwinding, upward, from her mother's still and lifeless body. When she regained her bearings, Sonya felt a sense of shock and comfort as she considered what it was she saw. Was this her mother's soul, leaving her body? To this day, Sonya is undergirded by a profound sense of peace when she recalls the image she saw, even as she wonders if she has become "mystic" or "strange."

In the encounter with death, nothing seems so clear as the fact that we are not sure what lies beyond death. In our grief it is inevitable that we will come up against the limitations of science and all human experience, and come into the realm of the metaphysical and the spiritual. For death *is* a door, but the question remains: A door to what?

Out of Our League

When I speak or think about death, I often feel like I do when the men of my household are assembling something, like a new computer table. They seem to have a nascent know-how for fitting this odd piece together with that unidentifiable piece, and making these unlikely bits of particle-board into something sturdy enough to hold up thousands of dollars worth of equipment. I could not do this if my life depended on it. I flee the area, to return and sit at my keyboard later, beholden to them and their, it would appear, inborn skills. But first I flee, I say, for one big reason: What they know puts something small and threatened inside of me on trial; makes me ask, fiercely, accusingly, why I cannot encounter a set of computer-table-assembly instructions without feeling lost and dumb.

When we encounter death profoundly, as at the death of a parent, most of us experience this same constellation of feelings. We feel mystified, stupefied, at a loss to account for it or to know what to think about it. For some of us, who thought we had solid beliefs, this can be a real shock. Despite the defined doctrines of our faith, whether it is a formal religion or one we have cobbled together ourselves, when death's door opens, we all tend to stand gaping at the reality of this stark, vacuous, black hole in the cosmos and think, "Faced with it, now I'm not sure what I really think."

Most of us have what we might call "back porch" or "Sunday school" beliefs about what lies beyond the door of death. These beliefs are pieced together out of conversations and philosophical meanderings on sunny days, in an atmosphere that is full of life and lively discussion. The conclusions we come to in these settings have about the same spiritual ballast as sports scores, gardening or cooking tidbits, or business or vacation plans that, a moment later, career down the bright-bubbling stream of conversation into which this most serious of subjects momentarily flowed. With no sense of death imminent, we form our beliefs about death with about the same depth as school kids chattering on about what they might be when they grow up.

We see death approaching, however, in the face of someone close to us, and suddenly it is a different matter. When the door opens, what will be on the other side? What happens after death? This is a subject on which not one of us can expound with any personal, firsthand experience. Call it belief. Call it religious doctrine; call it opinion based on listening to the anecdotal evidence, and doing a lot of reading on the subject. However strongly we utter what it is we have to say about what comes after life it is still, in scientifically provable terms, mere conjecture. If we are braver and more honest, we will admit that what we really have, down in our souls, are many more questions than answers. Is death only the end of the body? Or is death the end of the soul? And beyond that, is there a heaven? a hell? Or, do we come back in a cycle of incarnations? The truth is, in terms of ability to answer these questions definitively, we are way out of our league.

We Believe

We do not have anything like solid answers to any of the questions death poses, when it comes calling. We may be suddenly, painfully aware that what we think is what our culture or religion or those close to us have told us to think. What we know is *zip-ola*. What we are engaged in is, at best, educated guessing. Or, to put a spiritual spin on it, believing. And not only that, I think that every one of us also puts a personal spin on believing. So depending on how much or how little we have thought about it, what beliefs we formulate about ultimate matters, like death, are either clear or somewhat murky.

What we are all engaged in, then, is formulating a personal

belief. Some of us have been at this awhile, and others of us have only taken a light-hearted poke at it. What is it, exactly, or vaguely, that you believe about what lies beyond the door of death? For many of us, the idea of "heaven," with streets paved with gold, and angels, is a little too sketchy. Reuniting with dead loved ones is appealing. But after that . . . Hanging around on heavenly street corners lacks motivating force. As does hob-nobbing with angelic beings and going to one eternally-long worship service. Well, forgive me, but . . .oddly enough, the Christian faith, which is so explicit when it comes to certain dogmas, is weak on what awaits us in that long, long, long stretch of our lives we call eternity, so weak as to be fairly unuseful for many of us. What most people believe about life after life, after giving a respectful head nod to the heaven thing, seems to fall into one of several general categories.

Our Immortality Lies in Our Contribution

One member of my church expressed such excitement about the Habitat-for-Humanity house he and a team from our church were building, that I asked, why did he feel such intense, personal enthusiasm? "Because," he replied, "it means something I have done will live on after I die. And my greatest goal in life is to leave the earth better than I found it." His connection with the concept of immortality is a common one. He not only lives to build, he will continue to live in what he constructs. Others of us have a similar, if more warm and animated, view. Mothers have the deep sense that they will live on, not only in the fond the memories of their children, but in the way their children nurture other lives. Men dream deeply, not only of leaving their own marks on the world, but that they will raise sons and daughters who will mark the world as well.

A Cycle of Life and Death ... and Life

A second view of immortality, once an Eastern view, now more prevalent in the West, is that immortality is found in the cycle of life-death-life known as reincarnation. In this belief, our bodies pass back into the dust of the earth, but our souls are eternal, and so they migrate and enter another body at another time. Some Christian theologians and other Western thinkers who were once rigidly linear in their logic are now approaching the nonlinear beliefs of the East with interest. Some are finding a compatibility, even a sense of completion, in the concept of reincarnation.

The Unutterable Beauty of Now

Keats, the great Romantic poet, penned the thought: "Death is the mother of beauty." By that, Keats meant that because life is limited—and we all face the bitter end, called death—we should view life itself as unutterably beautiful. If there is no life after death, if death is nothingness for both body and soul, then life is our only immortality. This view, that both body and soul die together, is also a common one in our scientific age, with its demand that we produce measurable "proof" for everything. While on one hand, the concept that we have no eternal soul to survive us would seem to make life devoid of meaning and pleasure, some hold that just the opposite is true: My life's precious and unique beauty, and yours, lies in the fact that it will happen once, just once, and never again.

Each of these three basic views of immortality undergirds whole systems of belief. All three have merit. A sense that we achieve immortality based on what we contribute to the world has a humane ethic to it. And on a personal level we do not die so much as live on in a building, a trust fund, a mission, a business, or something as homey as a quilt that is passed on for generations.

Similar to this is the sense that we live on in our children, or, if we think in more broad-based humanitarian terms, in many, many children. On a personal level, our lives touch and flow into, and make better, other lives. Not monuments or organizations, but actual people are our immortal habitation.

A belief in reincarnation delivers the sense that our immortality is achieved on a super-social level. The survival of my soul is not about "me" per se, it is about moving on in endless and intimate connection with a fabric of "other" people. Beyond death's door lies a view of our connectedness to all things that is more intimate than the connection organ recipients sometimes sense with their donors. There is no real death, only a reconfiguring into new combinations. Death as the end—even this creates a sense of genuine, if fleeting, immortality. It does so by heightening our awareness of the present moment to a state of near-ecstasy. Each day, our whole life as an embodied soul, is eternal.

Personally, all three of these foundational concepts form my beliefs about what lies beyond death.

And before you leap to jump down my throat, let me assure you that I know these three basic belief structures contradict each other. "Life ends at death" cannot be true at the same time that "the soul is immortal" is true. And "the soul is reincarnated" cannot be true at the same time that "building a building, or leaving progeny is our immortality" is true. For me, and I know some will find this maddening, I prefer to rest my belief in a sense of contradiction. But I am comfortable in the realm of contradictions. It leaves me with a sense of openness and possibility. I can hang my hat on each of the three pegs, the possibility that death is a doorway to nothing, or to a cycle of successive lives, or that what I do here in this life is my only lasting memorial. Whereas others are sure of what they believe about what comes after death, the bottom line is, I just do not know at this point in my life what I believe, and

I prefer to remain in the state of humility that taking no sure position creates in me.

For me, belief means staying open to possibility. My "faith life" goes something like this: Sometimes I run with the Sonya's of the world and imagine something supernatural occurs at death. I believe more is going on than we can see when a soul departs a body. Because of my work as a pastor, I have witnessed the moment, dozens of times, when a soul departs the body. And though I do not see with Sonya's eyes, I see the difference between the body vital and the body devoid of its spark-like animating principle. It is in that distinct difference that I, for a moment, fleetingly, catch a glimpse of the soul. The soul is that which lights us up, and also that which goes out of us when we die. Thus, when I am inclined to come down on the supernatural side of things, dying is, to me, the soul's journey away from the body. Where it goes I cannot truthfully say I know.

Here is where I get in trouble with Christians who are "more sure," and even more adamant, about the soul's ultimate destiny. Whether our souls go to nothingness, or to another body, or to God, I just do not know. There is no way we can know. And sometimes I have to hold myself in-check a little, and keep myself from acting miffed toward people who feel they must know, demand to know. I wonder, with some confused amazement, why they think they are due an answer, when no one else on the planet, throughout all time, has been given a definite answer.

Let us take the matter into the realm of specifically Christian belief. I know the testimony of scripture tells us that there is a time after time. In the words of the Apostle Paul, we can be filled with the eternal spirit of God ". . . so that we too might walk in newness of life" (Rom. 6:4) meaning, with a sense of eternal life. Sometimes I have that "sense." Big. General. But I do not pretend to understand in the smallest part what life after death means. Even Jesus' declaration after his resurrection: "I am returning to my Father and your Father" (John 20:17) is, really, infuriatingly vague. "Returning to the Father?" What does that mean? Where is that? And what goes on there? (And please do not give me the streets of gold thing.) Perhaps you are wondering what I get out of doggedly holding on to a contradictory set of beliefs, other than an occasional dose of insecurity offset by a satisfying lack of smugness. I ask myself that, too.

Living with the Door Open

Deepak Chopra has been bugging the world lately with his idea that "we humans inhabit a minor galaxy in an enormous cosmos." He is trying to open us up to possibility. Many people have warmed to his idea of just how limited our concepts and beliefs really are. To me, he is saying, let's not approach our individual destinies with so much fear and apprehension, pumping so much significance into death itself, that we claw for answers, cling at answers, in an effort we call belief that is actually more of a scramble to control terror. If underneath our "belief" lies fear, and not an utter trust in a great Benevolence behind all things, where is the faith in that?

I, for my part, approach death the way I approach gardening. And in particular, the growing of sweetpeas, a flower I adore.

For years I have planted hard, smooth, beanlike seeds that are supposed to shoot up, I presume, like skyrockets into sweetpea plants laden with colorful blooms. Only in my case, what comes up are two little leafs and a string like tendril that reaches up briefly, then stops growing. Then every single green shoot withers yellow and dies. Something is just not right about this and I, for love or money, cannot figure it out. I assumed there was a deficiency in the soil, and loaded the garden with chicken manure. But, no luck. What my sweetpeas have taught me is that when things want to live, they live, and when they do not want to live, they do not. Why is a mystery. Whatever God wants, God gets. When it comes to the great matters, like life and death, they are beyond our province.

But, and here is the point, every year I plant sweetpeas. I have no idea why they will not grow. I have no idea why I continue to hope that this year they will not wither and die but rise spiritedly from the dead ground into the living air. But hope against hope is what I do. Quite apparently, something in me says: Sow the seed. Leave the door of possibility wide open. What you do not know will not hurt you. Who knows, when things finally break wide open, how beautiful it might actually be?

If it is not obvious to you by now, I need the open door kind of faith. My spirit thrives in images and possibilities, and withers in apologetics and hammered-down answers. I can tolerate lots of ambiguity and, no blot against you, perhaps you cannot. In the matter of beliefs about death and immortality you may want something less vague and more tangible, less reflect-on-able and more do-able. If that is so, this is the best I can offer you, and I offer it wholeheartedly.

Death is a great teacher, but not about itself. In my thinking, the most important and practical belief about death that we can hold is that, if we are wise, death can teach us about life.

Learning from Death about Life

That death is certain teaches us that every life is precious. Each life is a divine sowing into earth's soil, containing in its tight seed the possibility and the wonders of growth and fruition and blossoming. Death also teaches us that every breath of our own, individual lives is wonderful. Each breath allows us to live only for a moment. Each breath is the difference between life and death. The moment and our breath are really all we have. Death teaches us, then, to be alive in the moment, to live consciously aware of each moment, and every surrounding, and each person, taking them in the way we take in air and really experiencing who and what they are.

Death teaches us, too, that in order to enjoy this wonderful present-to-life consciousness we must let go of everything that would pitch us headlong out of the present, the angry or regretful memories that would suck us backwards into a past that is gone and cannot be changed, and also the worried, anxious imaginings that blast us away to a future that is not yet ours and may never be. Death says, "Do all your worries matter that much, that they should be allowed to steal your life this moment? Are your grudges and unforgiveness so important to hold on to, that they should eat at your soul's peace, your body's health, and your spirit's ability to vitally connect with other people?"

Death teaches us that, as long as we have breath in our bodies, we might as well contribute something to the world. What we contribute might as well be . . . us. You and me. The sowing of God, with wonderful ideas, gifts to give, love and vitality to spill and spill and spill. What are we waiting for? For what later moment that may not come are we holding back?

Will we, or won't we, live in the now?

Postlude

As it is for the dying, death is a door for us the living, too. Will it be a door that leads only to grief? Surely, it will lead us to our own experiences of grief. When we lose someone as close as a parent, we will experience the simple sadness that comes from losing the good, or complicated emotions that require long sorting, or an indifference that masks what we will not permit ourselves to feel. We will have to walk through whatever room of the soul grief leads us to. We may either skirt these places within ourselves, or work our way through what we find locked up there.

And beyond the work of grief, assuming we are brave and willing to do it, what will we find?

If we open ourselves wide enough, deep enough, when death comes knocking, we can discover, maybe for the first time, the shape and texture of our true beliefs. These may have a most definite form, and be supported by chapter and verse. Or, they may be ambiguous, contradictory, and open. What we find, if we allow death to bring us around, present to ourselves, is—oddly, amazingly, wonderfully enough—our belief about life. And if we are wise, our belief in life. Life that cannot, ultimately, be controlled. Life that in fact bucks control.

As a pastor, I have prayed for desperately ill people, and seen them die. As a gardener, I have toiled and sweated to amend soil so that seeds may grow, and what has sprung up has withered and died. I greatly fear, I deeply dislike, death and loss. But more than death, I fear living a life that is no life. I fear living in a way that tries to control, and guarantee completely, that living will be exactly what I want it to be, on schedule, beautifully blooming always, with no risks and no losses. And I, for one, will not live an unlived life.

For us the living, death can be the door through which we enter to embrace life, maybe more fully than we ever have before. Embrace it, I say, because it is a blessed uncertainty. A gift that blossoms each moment, wonderfully alive, alive, alive. Each breath a step that moves us on to the spiritual maturity that does not demand answers, but is vibrantly present to the people and the work of the moment.

May we, you and I, live in this growing maturity until the moment we do die. The moment when we step through death's door and find that we are alive again . . . in some other kind of life, the likes of which are only a mystery to us now.

Eight

Do This

IN THE YEAR THAT FOLLOWS A parent's death, we will be active. The activities that go on take place inwardly and outwardly. We go through the interior shifts that we have been exploring here. We will take care of their many legal and business affairs; we will distribute their clothing and possessions. The family will slowly regroup, and a new patriarch or matriarch may emerge. We are like spiders whose beautifully-patterned webs have been torn. We rebuild. We redesign. Emotionally, spiritually, physically, we work our way through.

Listen to William Sloan Coffin Jr's words: "When a parent dies, as did my mother last month, they take with them a large portion of the past . . . and we become the latest recruit in the world's army of the beloved." Indeed, the world we now face is changed because we are changed. We are asked to make something of the past, to sort it, and understand it, and determine which aspects of it we will leave behind, and which we will weave into the present. At the same moment we are asked to give thought to the kind of future we will now make, given a glimpse of our mortality.

Though the purpose of this book has been to help you explore the inner road through grief to greater and more settled maturity, I would be remiss if I did not close by looking at what I consider to be the most important tasks we can accomplish in the first year after losing a parent.

Focus on Inner Work

Many of us get through a loss by focusing on all the practical tasks that need to be done. Skimming the surface passes for "getting through it." To be sure, there are lists of duties to be done. And yet the most important tasks, when it comes to our human experiences, are not the practical ones. Rather, they are the inner works of sorting out, shifting with changes, and becoming. The primary task of every one of us is to determine, and keep determining who we are as individuals, as life shifts around us. Losing our parents is a huge shift. In the year after that loss we may need to ask: What parts of me need to be let go, that is, what sense of duty or obligation did I take on, because my parents pressed it upon me, as if it were my own? What did I inherit from them that is now truly mine, warped-and-woofed into my own true nature? And also what genuine interests and passions have I ignored or suppressed for some reason as long as they were alive?

Important Dates and Holidays

Seven months after her father's death, in late winter, Mae found herself slumping into the blues for no apparent reason. As she talked this through with her spiritual director a reason became clear. Around March twentieth or twenty-first, the first day of spring, her father always invited her over for coffee and pie, and to flip through seed catalogs, so they could plan their gardens together. It was their special event. And Mae now realized that her "blues" had set in when she flipped up the February calendar page with its picture of a snowy stream, to reveal the March page with its picture of seedlings bursting through the earth. The moment she made this connection, Mae burst into tears of grief for her father.

It is likely that during your first year of loss, collateral losses will occur to you, as well. Mother will not be coming up to camp and playing Monopoly with the children. Dad will no longer be donning the silly red stocking cap and playing Santa's helper. That special card or call will not be coming on your, or your children's birthdays. Keeping a good journal during the first year, along with keeping an eye on the calendar, may help you face and deal with your loss as it echoes down through the first year. You may want to mark the first anniversary of your parents' deaths, and maybe even more importantly, mark their birthdays and wedding anniversarys. It may also be important to you to mark any days that were "special" to your parents. For instance, my mother always remembers the day of her mother's death. At her death, I will want to incorporate the dates she honored into my year as a way of remembering and honoring her. Keeping track of the calendar can help us anticipate dates that might, otherwise "sneak up" on us and catch us emotionally unprepared. Many people find they are overwhelmed at how acutely they feel their loss on special days, and managing these unhappy surprises can be important.

Allowing Relationships to Shift

With the death of a parent our relationships with family members will shift, perhaps even dramatically. Greg was never close to his father or brothers, while his mother was alive. For some reason, she was a kind of emotional and spiritual hub whom they each related to, but they never did much to work on their relationships with each other. Upon her death, they had a lot of reconsidering to do. Did they want to get to know each other better, and stay close? Death is a great time to begin or renew these relationships, and to do so requires us to

Do This

be intentional about it. What kind of relationship do we want? Perhaps it is time to say to the brother or sister with whom we have been at odds, or distant, "I know we haven't been close, but I think it's time to change that." Perhaps it is time to say to our surviving parent, if we have had big differences, "Maybe it's time we ironed-out our problems. What do you say?"

Allow Others to Grieve in Their Own Ways

Each of us experiences loss differently. Grief hits us at different times. Jayne saw her brother, Warren, become cool and business-like when their mother died, and concluded he just did not care. Two months later, in a conversation with his wife, Jayne commented bitterly, "Mom's death doesn't even mean a thing to Warren." Warren's wife lashed back, "How can you possibly say that? He drove himself like a madman for six weeks, tying up all her affairs, and then he crashed. He's been talking to our priest, and seeing a doctor for depression."

We must always remember to be respectful of the way another person processes grief. We must also respect the fact that, though they related to the same person we have lost, their relationship was not identical to ours. Individuality, temperament, and experience are all factors, and so some family members will cope much better and others less well. If we have the extra energy, it may be helpful to be a helper, even if we think we have nothing much to offer. With grieving family members and friends, I often say: "I'm just going to stay close. Do you mind if I call you more often than I usually do?" Being there, and allowing someone else to go through their own process of grief, may be a great gift that helps build the relationship in new ways.

As an important side note: If young children are affected

by the loss, mark your calendar for six months from the time of the death. Most children experience delayed reactions to the death of a beloved parent or grandparent. Six months is roughly when reality hits home. That is when those who love these children need to be on the alert and ready to be available and tender.

Support the Surviving Parent with Care and Respect

Oftentimes, a surviving parent needs help, care, or support of one kind or another. David discovered that, since his mother had always taken care of financial matters, his father did not even know how to deposit a check in their bank account. Kelly's mother felt overwhelmed at the thought of household repairs and maintenance. If we have a surviving parent, he or she may need help figuring out how to replace practical activities the other partner normally performed. As parents age, needs may become more acute. We may find that the surviving parent is actually not able to take care of necessary duties. Jeri found that her mother, who was otherwise healthy and able to care for herself, simply could not handle organizing a budget and paying bills. Nick's father loved his home and did well on his own, but because of a heart condition he was not able to do the snow shoveling his wife used to do.

We must carefully assess what part of a surviving parent's burden we are able to pick up. Distance and finances may or may not allow us, realistically, to do what we might like to do. Or if a parent needs special attention, such as in-home health or hygienic care, we may or may not, realistically, be able to add those duties to our own life-load. As much as possible, I believe it is important to involve a surviving parent in making decisions about his/her care and support.

Well-meaning as it might seem, to rush in and take over,

Do This

it may also be obtrusive and surprisingly unwelcome. A first rule of thumb: Ask. "If you would like some help with . . . I would be happy to" is the way to approach these matters. A second rule of thumb is: Do not offer help that you cannot, or are really not willing to, follow through on. Or, better put: If you offer, make it a priority to follow through.

Offering practical support might mean listening and helping a surviving parent redesign his/her future. Keep in mind that remaking a life is a slow process. Do not push your parent to make hasty decisions. When we do that, it is usually for our own convenience, or because we are uncomfortable with things in limbo. It is important not to overdo care for the surviving parent. He or she must be encouraged to take charge where they can. The point is both for you as bereaved adult child and the parent as widow or widower to return to life after someone has died. But there are decisions to be made at different times of the year. I like to encourage people not to let themselves get overwhelmed by trying to figure everything out all at once, but to allow the decisions to come at them season by season, through fall, summer, winter, spring.

Know When You and Others Need Support

Grief for a person who is important to us is a spiritual pilgrimage through time and seasons. It will come at us in phases, and the phases are often different. Anger will come. Loneliness will come. Immobility will come. Depression will come. They may go away only to return . . . then go away for good. Sometimes, though, they will come and stay. If we begin to pick up signs that we, or someone close to us, are stuck in some emotional distress, the earlier we seek help the better.

Signs that someone is stuck in an emotional rut include: chronic anger; fear; loneliness; panic; lack of feelings; lack of motivation; physiological changes like severe weight loss or gain; insomnia; indigestion; regressive behavior; the voicing of grandiose plans not executed; mental disorganization; increased use of medicines or alcohol or drugs; guilt and self-blame; repetitive stories from the past, with no future-focus.

Help can come in various forms. Support groups exist in many communities for people who are going through loss. They are magnificent aids as they reaffirm what we know about life. We are not alone in our grief. Groups can be useful in lifting our spirits enough to allow our own coping skills to gain in strength and effectiveness. Professionals, like social service counselors, pastors, or psychologists, are also a source of help. They can often assess needs better than someone close to the situation, not just because they are objective but because we often disclose troublesome details to professionals more readily than to family members or friends, whom we may fear burdening. A professional is also more likely to provide a kind of compassionate but therapeutic "toughness" when it is time to apply a little pressure to help the struggler stop resisting help and move on.

Allow Yourself a Vacation from Grief

Sometimes several months into a time of grief we may feel overweighted, restless, snappish, disgruntled. This is often a signal that grief has been too much with us. We need not abandon our process. But we can allow ourselves a little time-off from it. What we need is something like a vacation. Maybe exactly like a vacation. Especially, if we have been the primary caregiver, we absolutely need to get away from the setting we have been in and get a look at new vistas, not to mention a good rest. Inwardly, we may also need the equivalent of a vacation, again, especially if we have been the care giver. Whether we need a professional to tell us, or we are able to do this for ourselves, we need to hear, inside, "You are relieved of the duties, tasks, and responsibilities you took on, on behalf of your parent. Job well done." Odd as it may seem, we do need these inner markers to let us know when our task is complete. That is, when we can "vacate" a role we have filled.

Focus on the Future

Difficult as it is to sense when we have lost someone as deeply loved as a parent, life is going on.

The river that is our own life does flow on, whether we are taking part in it or sitting distant from it in our grief. Sometimes it is not that we do not want to go on, we just don't know how.

"I know the plans I have for you," says the Lord, through the prophet Jeremiah, "plans to give you . . . a hope and a future" (Jer. 29:11). For all of our lives, perhaps, whether we have lived just across town or across an ocean, we have always had a conscious or unconscious sense that the parents we loved were there to love and care for us when needed. Now they are gone. And those who bent benevolently over the cradle of our infancy, counseled the gaffs of our youth, soothed the emotional turbulence of our adulthood, have been removed. Deep inside we are tempted to feel we are alone out in the cold universe. The time right after a parent dies is, in fact, a wonderful time to renew or begin a deeper relationship with God. To do so is to open ourselves, as the prophet records, to hope and to the future. God, the Source of life, yours and mine, is also the God of today and tomorrow.

My prayer for you, in closing, is that you will move through grief and find greater maturity in spirit. That you will sift the past for the gold, and the gifts of character, that are there for you. That you will find "enough" of the blessings that were granted to you, along with "enough" forgiveness to release you from your hurts, that could otherwise bind you and keep you from growing for the rest of your life. Finally, I pray that you will take a new step in your life's journey. A step toward God, the One who knows what the future holds, and the One who holds the future. I pray that beyond this grief, perhaps because you have taken the time to explore grief, your future will be full of the compassion and wisdom that come from a buoyant spirit. Amen.